SCHÖNING´S TRAVEL GUIDES

BERLIN
AND
POTSDAM

Text and concept: Bernhard Schneidewind · **Translation:** C. Watson
Photos: Bildarchiv Lenartz, R. Carow, S. Cordes, Deutsche Luftbild, Deutsche-Presse-Agentur, F 1 online, U. Findeisen, G. A. F. F.-Fotoarchiv, S. Gödecke, F. Heinze-von Hippel KG, S. Jacob, I. Janicek, P. Kanicki, N. Krüger, F. Kübler, U. Latza, W. Okon, W. Otto, F. Mader, J. Reetz, S. Rehberg, C. Reinhard, Fa. Schikkus, G. Schneider, E. Schröder, M. Schürmann, H. Wanke, W. Weber
Our thanks to the Association of the Friends of Prussian Palaces and Gardens Berlin-Brandenburg for their friendly support and cooperation.
Graphic design: Schöning Studio · **Cartography:** Pharus-Verlag
Editorial staff: R. Dohrmann Schöning-Verlag

Distributed by: SCHIKKUS · Otto-Suhr-Alle 114 · 10585 Berlin
Overall production and © Copyright by
SCHÖNING & CO + GEBRÜDER SCHMIDT
An der Hülshorst 5 · 23568 LÜBECK
☎ (04 51) 310 3-0 · Fax (04 51) 3 52 83
E-mail: info@schoening-verlag.de
Internet: www.schoening-verlag.de
ISBN: 3-89917-145-4

ROUTES

Berlin

Potsdam

BERLIN

Eight routes
to take to
discover the city

A pocket travel guide for people making a quick visit to Berlin can hardly be an A–Z of the city: Berlin is far too large and diverse to be covered by handy travel guides. And who would ever go to Berlin to read long books about the city there?

Here's the answer: a guide to Berlin in seven chapters, plus as bonus the town of palaces and gardens, Potsdam.

BERLIN

ROUTE 7

ROUTE 6

ROUTEN 1 2 3 4 5

Pankow

Berliner Ring

Mitte

Marzahn-

Kreuzberg

Hellersdorf

Tempelhof

Neukölln

Müggelsee

Steglitz

Köpenick

Schönefeld

Dresden

endorf

orf

The areas coloured in the general map are reproduced as a colour index on the right edge of the pages. A table of contents is given on the inside front cover and an index at the end of the guide (from p. 142).

Each chapter is supplemented by a section with useful addresses (on eating & drinking, shopping, sights, leisure, after eight), intended to encourage readers to explore the city.

Where was the Wall?

Even with this barrier, it wasn't clear who was in front of it and who behind.

But it was certainly clear that it existed and how it was erected.

Its construction began on August 13th 1963 and its demolition on November 9th 1989.

It had a length of 155 km (43.1 km between East and West Berlin, 111.9 km between West Berlin and East Germany). It encompassed the three western sectors and skirted the former urban district boundaries. The off-limits border areas were up to 100 metres wide. 37 km cut through residential areas, 17 km through industrial areas, 30 km through forest, 24 km through water areas, 54 km over railway embankments, through fields, marshy areas, etc.

The Wall put an end to transit traffic on eight city transit (S-Bahn) lines and four underground lines. It intersected 192 main and side streets, 97 of which led to East Berlin and 95 to the GDR.

On the East German side, there were 300 watchtowers, 22 bunkers, 256 guard dog patrol areas.

The Wall consisted of a four metre high concrete slab wall (107.3 km) with 45,000 individual segments, each weighing 2.75t, or an up to four metre high metal lattice-work fence (65.3 km) – or both at quite a few places.

After the opening of the Wall, a small number of segments were auctioned off and clumps were sold by swarms of "Wall woodpeckers". The rest was pulverized and some of the material used for road building.

Small sections of the Wall have been retained at only six locations in the city area.

The Wall 1961–1989

Border between West and East Berlin

Border crossing points
1 Bornholmer Strasse
2 Chausseestrasse
3 Invalidenstrasse
4 Friedrichstrasse
   Checkpoint Charlie
5 Heinrich-Heine-Strasse
6 Oberbaumbrücke
7 Sonnenallee

Reinickendorf
Pankow
Hohen-schön-hausen
Weißen-see
Wedding
Prenz-lauer-berg
Spandau
Tier-garten
MITTE
Fried-richs-hain
Marzahn
Charlottenburg
Kreuz-berg
Lichten-berg
Hellers-dorf
Sectors of the Western Allies
Wilmersdorf
Schöne-berg
Soviet sector
Zehlendorf
Steglitz
Tempel-hof
Neukölln
Treptow
Köpenick

BERLIN DURING THE COLD WAR

A guide

Anyone visiting Berlin generally already knows what they are letting themselves in for: Berlin is big, Berlin is noisy, Berlin is fast, Berlin is chaotic and, above all, Berlin is a permanent building site. This city is being newly invented, newly planned, newly built day by day. Not that that's anything new – it's precisely what's characteristic of Berlin: it's not there, it's always just becoming.

Berlin is a young city historically. When the first crude huts of wood and clay were erected here in the middle of the swampy Spree meadowlands, there were already for example in Italy buildings of permanent materials several stories high with real doors, windows and roofs. But at that time modest settlements developed here between marshes and Brandenburg sand on this and the far side of the Spree, Berlin and Cölln. At the beginning of the 14th c., these combined and took shelter behind a joint city wall on the site of the present Nikolai Quarter to protect themselves against the tender mercies of marauding competing dynasties. The settlement grew slowly but constantly, becoming the capital of Brandenburg, but was devastated by the plague epidemics in the 16th c. and the fighting during the Thirty Years' War in the 17th c. From then on, however, it grew by leaps and bounds without suffering setbacks. Its significance increased and its population grew, Berlin becoming first capital of Prussia, then capital of the German Empire and finally at the beginning of the 20th c. a European metropolis between Moscow and Paris.

Berlin is a city of modern times and the modern age, but the vicissitudes of history – the first world war, the National Socialist dictatorship, the second world war followed by the division of Germany and the city itself – cruelly disappointed all the great hopes that were continually placed in it.

Since 1990, Berlin has again been completely reinvented, though the various inventors have been at odds with one another, some wanting to see Berlin as it used to be, others preferring a future-oriented city. As this dispute can't be decided by anyone arbitrarily, however, both a retrospective and a preview are being created at one and the same time – with turbulent life that is noisy, fast and chaotic in between.

This guide provides a fast, concise orientation through the supposed chaos of Berlin, presenting the city in seven lavishly illustrated sections – spotlighting the main sights in the east and west, north and south, as well as informing the visitor of pubs and restaurants, department stores and boutiques, theatres and swimming pools, discotheques and bars.

And our guide is also an invitation to visit Potsdam, said to be only the comma that has added itself on to Berlin, though that isn't true: the small town on the Havel lakes is, rather, the exclamation mark for the metropolis on the Spree. Anyone who doesn't know Potsdam, who's never seen the palaces and gardens, can't understand Berlin.

ROUTE 1

Berlin

CENTRE EAST

From Brandenburger Tor to Schlossbrücke

HIGHLIGHTS

1 BRANDENBURGER TOR
S BUS Unter den Linden

2 CHECKPOINT CHARLIE
U BUS Kochstrasse

3 GENDARMENMARKT
U BUS Stadtmitte

4 UNTER DEN LINDEN
U Französische Strasse
BUS Unter den Linden

5 STATE OPERA HOUSE
U Französische Strasse
BUS Neue Wache

6 NEUE WACHE
U Französische Strasse
BUS Neue Wache

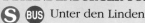

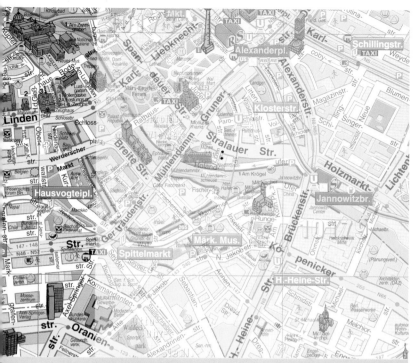

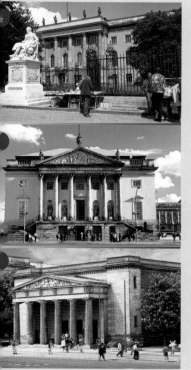

The historic city centre, stretching all the way from Pariser Platz to Kupfergraben, from the Spree to Kochstrasse, was created between the late 17th c. and late 19th c.

PUBLIC TRANSPORT

Unter den Linden:

S 1, S 2, S 25, S 26, Bus TXL, 100, 200, 348

Kochstrasse:

U 6, Bus 129

Französische Strasse:

U 6, Bus 147, 257

City centre:

U 2, U 6, Bus TXL, 147, 148

Neue Wache:

Bus 100, 200, 348

Brandenburger Tor, built in 1789-91 according to plans by Carl Gotthard Langhans

Brandenburger Tor isn't just a structure with a Viktoria in a four-horse chariot on top and five passages at ground level: it marks the centre of the city and the state. Brandenburger Tor is indeed a symbol, both for Berlin and for Germany as a whole, opening up the way to the west and providing access to the routes to the east. As if that had always been so.

Quadriga on Brandenburger Tor, a work by the sculptor Johann Gottfried Schadow

Brandenburger Tor was inaugurated in 1791 without ceremony. Its method of construction was clumsy: the sandstones were held together with cheese cement, the coating was simple – just whitewash – and the cost of construction reasonable, namely 110,902 talers, 20 groschens and 10 pfennigs. The **quadriga** was completed two years later and has since crowned the gate with three interruptions. In 1806, Napoleon had the quadriga, embossed in copper, packed into twelve crates and taken off to Paris as booty. Eight years later, it was retaken by Prussian troops. The quadriga was very badly damaged in the second world war. A copy was made in 1958 from a plaster cast of the original in a West Berlin workshop and at the end of September of the same year mounted on Brandenburger Tor – without the symbols of victory, the eagle and the iron cross on the staff held by the Viktoria. The work was last dismantled in March 1990, after

the Academy of Arts. But five years later, this area, which was created in 1734 during the extension of Friedrichstadt and also named a square up to 1814, was like an enormous building site. It began with the building of **Hotel Adlon** modelled on the former Adlon at this location. Today only the area south of the gate is yet to be developed: the US Embassy will be built there and, on the far side of Behrenstrasse, the **Memorial for the Murdered Jews of Europe**, which has been the subject of dispute for almost twenty years.

Only after completion of these projects will the square and its surroundings receive their final form. Then we'll be able to decide how the strife between the city planners at the beginning of the 1990s concerning the future of Potsdamer Platz has been decided: some wanted a square fit for a world city, others an entrance hall into the parlour of Berlin, into its new and at the same time old centre. But it's already certain that the square and, above all, the passages through Brandenburger Tor are reserved for pedestrians and cyclists only.

having been partially destroyed on New Year's Eve night of 1989–90. On August 6th 1991, the quadriga was then back at its place, this time with the victory symbols and without the flag-staff at the back of the goddess of victory installed by the GDR after the building of the Wall in autumn 1961.

In 1991, **Pariser Platz** in front of Brandenburger Tor still had nothing of its present character: it was a rectangular area with a garland of two rows of trees, featuring on its edge only the not particularly handsome building of

British Embassy (left) and Hotel Adlon (above) on Pariser Platz

Unter den Linden, the city-centre boulevard, 1.5 km long and up to 60 metres wide. The equestrian sculpture of Friedrich II is on the central reserve, very near the Neue Wache (1818) by Karl-Friedrich Schinkel (below).

At one end there's Brandenburger Tor, at the other the site of what used to be Berlin Palace. And in between the boulevard **Unter den Linden**, which expanded from the palace westwards in line with the rise of Prussia and its kings. Its

predecessor was a riding and hunting path leading from the palace to the electoral Tiergarten, created by Elector Johann Georg in 1573.

The avenue between Schlossplatz and Friedrichstrasse was given its present design mainly under the regency of Friedrich II. From 1740, he built the **Opera House** (1741–43), **St. Hedwig Cathedral** (1747–78) and **Royal Library** (1775–80) on the southern side of the street and on the northern side Prinz Heinrich Palace (1748–53) – today seat of **Humboldt Univer-**

sity – and thereby along with the **Armoury** (1706) created a group of buildings of feudal splendour, supplemented in 1818 by the **Neue Wache** by Karl Friedrich Schinkel as a demonstration of Prussian might and culture. Today the equestrian sculpture of Friedrich II by Christian Daniel Rauch on the central reserve of the boulevard watches over his work, which after reconstruction following the second world war is meanwhile a unique set of buildings in the city.

Sculpture of Humboldt in front of the university named after him

Operncafé in former Princesses Palace

On August 18th 1910, Wilhelmine Berlin paid tribute to Franz Joseph I, Emperor of Austria and King of Hungary, on his 80th birthday by naming the square between the Deutsche Staatsoper and Royal Library as well as the section of street in front after him. The square had been conceived as **Forum Fridericianum** 170 years previously by the newly crowned Friedrich II to demonstrate royalty's affinity with art and science. It was planned to build an **opera house**, an academy building and a royal palace here, but only the opera house was completed according to a design by Wenzeslaus von Knobelsdorff. A **library** was built instead of an academy and a princely palace instead of a royal palace.

The square sadly achieved fame on May 10th 1933, when the books of undesirable writers and thinkers

were burnt here, as elsewhere in National Socialist Germany. This act of barbarism is today recalled by an underground memorial by Micha Ullmann in the centre of the square, which has borne its present name since 1947.

St. Hedwig's Cathedral, which Knobelsdorff designed according to directions given by Friedrich II, is on the edge of **Bebelplatz**. "Build it like this," Friedrich II is said to have instructed Knobelsdorff, whereupon he turned a teacup upside down. Who can deny that this might have been true?

South of Unter den Linden:
St. Hedwig's Cathedral (left) at Bebelplatz, Friedrichswerder church (right) and the new foreign ministry (far right)

Bebelplatz beween the Deutsche Staatsoper and the Old Library

But it is certain that the building is modelled on the Pantheon in Rome. To the south-east of this church of the Catholic see of Berlin is the **Friedrichswerder church**, built close on 100 years later according to plans by Karl Friedrich Schinkel. This finely limbed, neo-Gothic brick building today serves as an exhibition venue for sculptures of the 16th–19th c.

Between the Friedrichswerder church and the transparent, light new building of the **foreign ministry**, there is a freshly built corner that recalls that the **Building Academy**, also designed by Schinkel, was located here until into the post-war era before being pulled down to make way for the GDR foreign ministry, which was for its part demolished after 1990.

Friedrichstrasse between the two world wars

At the dawn of the 20th c., there were about 20 Friedrichstrassen on the area of the present Berlin. Some of these streets were named after all the Friedrichs who had up to then played an important role in Prussian and German history as electors, kings or even emperors. Many of them were renamed between 1933 and 1938 because the Reich Chancellor and Führer Adolf Hitler wouldn't tolerate the company of any electors, kings or even emperors. Others lost their name around 1950 because the GDR, the workers' and farmers' state, didn't consider it opportune to pay homage to electors, kings or even emperors in whatever form. Today there are still three Friedrichstrassen in the whole of Berlin: one in Lichterfelde, one in Spandau and finally the famous one through the districts Mitte and Kreuzberg, though it's no longer what it used to be.

Since the end of the second world war, Kurt Tucholsky's jest in the turbulent 1920s that every Berliner would like to live out in front in Friedrichstrasse and behind out on the Baltic has been only a meaningless bon mot. The street that is today 3.3 km long was created in 1705 as the main axis of the new Friedrichstadt, named after Friedrich I, the first Prussian king, between Oranienburger Tor in the north and Mehringplatz in the south. It was almost completely destroyed in the war and with it the turbulent life there must have

Friedrichstrasse today, a chic and fashionably elegant shopping street

been at the city transit station and at the crossings Under den Linden and Leipziger Strasse – a real magnet for cafés, restaurants, variety shows and clubs.

Today, this Friedrichstrasse is still being reinvented. Some smart and interesting new buildings, such as the department store **Galeries Lafayette** by the architect Jean Nouvel at the corner with Französische Strasse and the neighbouring **Quartiere 206 and 207** between Friedrichstrasse and Gendarmenmarkt, have been built, but the real attraction of the street nowadays is a little sentry house on the central reserve between Zimmer- and Kochstrasse. This was where, just before the southern end of Friedrichstrasse, the border between East and West ran, this was where the Wall was with the third crossing from the US to the Soviet sector, **Checkpoint Charlie**, after Helmstedt (= Alpha) and Dreilinden (= Beta). The crossings were named after the US phonetic alphabet.

The nearby **Wall Museum** also has an exhibition on the history of this little stretch of Friedrichstrasse, which was frequently a focal point of world affairs during the Cold War era.

Checkpoint Charlie on Friedrichstrasse between Leipziger Strasse and Kochstrasse

Gendarmenmarkt with the German (left) and French Cathedral and the former Schauspielhaus between the two sacred buildings

City squares are seldom created on the basis of a single plan: they grow and develop to take on a shape at some time as if they had always been like that. Gendarmenmarkt, created around 1700 with the extension of Friedrichstadt east of Friedrichstrasse, gained its present form only with the completion of the **Schauspielhaus** designed by Karl Friedrich Schinkel in 1821.

Since then, its blend of intimacy and spaciousness has justifiably earned it the reputation of being one of Berlin's fine squares. It received its name – which derives from the cuirassier regiment Gens d´Armes, the armed bodyguard of the king that was stationed here – only in 1799. It was previously called Neuer Markt, Mittelmarkt, Friedrichstädtischer Markt, Schiller-

Altar area in French Cathedral

platz and Platz der Akademie. It acquired its present form under Friedrich II: the king had the horse stables on the square removed in 1773 to be replaced by a "French Comödienhaus". The grand "twin" buildings, the **German Cathedral** in the south and the **French Cathedral** in the north of the square, were built between 1780 and 1785. The Comödienhaus tended to be ignored. A new building completed in 1802 according to a design by Carl Gotthard Lang-

hans burnt down in 1817. The Schauspielhaus, now used for concerts, was built on its site up to 1821 according to plans by Karl Friedrich Schinkel. The **Schiller Monument** in front of the flight of steps of the Schauspielhaus was ceremoniously unveiled on November 10th 1871, the writer's 112th birthday. The foundation stone for the monument, a work by the sculptor Reinhold Begas, had, however, been laid the evening before Schiller's 100th birthday.

Gendarmenmarkt with the Schiller Monument in nocturnal illumination

buildings in the square formed by Leipziger-, Wilhelm-, Niederkirchner- and Stresemannstrasse. The former **Reich Aviation Ministry** with its 2,000 rooms, which was inaugurated in 1936 as the first major building of the German Reich and now accommodates the federal finance ministry, is on Wilhelmstrasse. Behind this building is the complex of the former Prussian manor house on Leipziger Strasse, today seat of the **Bundesrat** (Upper House), and the former Prussian state parliament, today seat of the Berlin **Chamber of Deputies**. This is opposite **Martin-Gropius-Bau** (1881), named after its builder, once arts and crafts school and today a venue for exhibitions, on the other side of Niederkirchnerstrasse. To the east of this, behind some remains of the Wall, is the **Topography of Terror** recalling the crimes of the Gestapo, which was based here.

The southern edge of the city centre is simply plastered with historic, cultural or architectural highlights, beginning in the west with the

Close neighbours: the former Prussian state parliament (left, above), today the Berlin Chamber of Deputies, Martin-Gropius-Bau (left, centre), venue of various exhibitions and the ruin of Anhalter station (below), recalling former transport arteries.

The ruin of **Anhalter Bahnhof** and the new building of the **Tempodrom** is south of this complex. The copy of the former **Spittelkolonnaden** on Leipziger Strasse in the middle of the high-rise building blocks from the GDR era is near the beautiful baroque building in Lindenstrasse, which served as Berlin Museum for a long time but has now been linked up with the **Jewish Museum** (designed by Daniel Libeskind) built right next to it.

On the eastern end of this string of pearls there is finally **Märkisches Museum**, built in the style of a medieval monastery, and the neighbouring **Ermeler House**, a baroque edifice painstakingly reconstructed both outside and inside.

Attractions on the southern edge of Friedrichstadt: the avant-garde Tempodrom (above, right), Märkisches Museum (right centre) near Jannowitzbrücke and the Jewish Museum (below), the most spectacular new building in Berlin after reunification

Adresses in Centre East

Eating & drinking

Café Tucher, Pariser Platz 6a,
daily 9–1, Tel: 22 48 94 64
Artists' club Die Möwe
Palais am Festungsgraben
Restaurant open daily from 19.30
Tel: 204 37 99
LebensArt, Unter den Linden 69a,
Mon.–Thurs. 7–23, Fr. 7–24, Sat.
9–24 and Sun. 9–23, Tel: 229 00 18
Newton-Bar, Charlottenstrasse 57,
Sun.–Thurs. 10–3, Fr. and Sat.
10–4, Tel: 202 95 40
Operncafé, Unter den Linden 5,
daily 8–24, Tel: 20 26 83
Porta Brandenburgo
Wilhelmstrasse 87/88,
Italian and Japanese cuisine, daily
11.30–23.30, Tel: 229 95 87
Refugium
Auf dem Gendarmenmarkt 5,
Mon.–Thurs., 10–24, Fr. and Sat.
10–1, Sun. 11–24, cuisine until 23,
Tel: 229 16 61
Sale e Tabacchi, Kochstrasse 18,
Italian cuisine, Mon.–Fr. 8–24, Sat.
and Sun. 12–24, Tel: 252 11 55
Tadshikische Teestube (tea rooms)
Am Festungsgraben 1, Mon.–Fr.
17–24, Sat. 11–15, Tel: 204 11 12

Shopping

Anastasia, Russian market
Reinhardtstrasse 8, Mon.–Fr. 9–19,
Sat. 9–15.30, Tel: 28 04 69 64
Buchhandlung Raduga (bookshop)
Friedrichstrasse 176/179
Russian books
Mon.–Fr. 11–18.30, Sat. 12–16,
Tel: 20 30 23 21
Budapester Schuhe (shoes)
Friedrichstrasse 81, Tel: 20 38 8110
Galeries Lafayette
Friedrichstrasse 76-78
Mon–Fr. 9–20, Sat. 9–16,
Tel: 20 94 80 www.otw-lafayette.de
Kulturkaufhaus Dussmann
Friedrichstrasse 90,
Mon–Sat. 10–22, Tel: 20 25 0
www.dussmann.de

Store with delivery service for left-
handed persons at "Dussmann"
Dorotheenstrasse 39,
Mon.–Fr. 10–20, Sat. 10–18,
Tel: 39 10 09 22
Parliamentary bookshop
Wilhelmstrasse 68 a,
Mon.–Thurs. 7.30–18, Fr. 7.30–16,
Tel: 22 48 95 44
Quartier 205, Friedrichstrasse 67,
Mon.–Fr. 10–20,Sat. 10–16,
Tel: 20 94 54 00,
Extended opening hours
for restaurant
The British Bookshop
Mauerstrasse 83-84, Mon.–Fr.
10–19, Sat. 10–14, Tel: 238 46 80
Trödelmarkt am Zeughaus (flea
market), Sat./Sun.

Sights

Checkpoint Charlie and
Wall Museum
Friedrichstrasse 43-44
daily 9–22,Tel: 253 72 50
Deutscher Dom
(German Cathedral)
Gendarmenmarkt 1
Exhibition on German
history, Tues.–Sun. 10–18,
Tel: 202 26 90
German Historic Museum
in Armoury, Unter den Linden 2,
Tues.–Thurs. 10–18, Thurs. –22,
Tel: 20 30 40, www.dhm.de
Französischer Dom
(French Cathedral)
Gendarmenmarkt 5
Tues.–Sat. 12–17
Sun. 11–17, Tel: 229 17 60
Outlook balustrade open from
April, Glockenspiel daily 10, 12,
14 and 16
Friedrichswerder church
Werderscher Markt, Tues.–Sun.
10–18, Tel: 208 13 23
Hemp Museum, Mühlendamm 5
Tues.–Fr. 10–20, Sat./Sun. 12–20,
Tel: 242 48 27

Hugenot Museum in
French Cathedral
Gendarmenmarkt 5, Tues.–Sat.
12–17, Sun. and public holidays
11–17, Tel: 229 17 60
Berlin information and
documentation centre of the
federal commissioner for GDR
state security police documents
Mauerstrasse 38, Mon.–Sat. 10–18,
Tel: 23 24 79 51
Jewish Museum
Lindenstrasse 14, daily 10–20,
Mon. –22, Tel: 25 99 34 10
Märkisches Museum
Am Köllnischen Park 5
Tues.–Sun. 10–18, Tel: 30 86 60
Martin-Gropius-Bau
Niederkirchnerstrasse 7
Various exhibitions
Tues.–Fr. and Sun. 10–20,
Sat. 10–22, Tel: 25 48 60
Museum of Things (Werkbund Archive) in Martin-Gropius-Bau
Niederkirchnerstrasse 7,
Wed.–Mon. 10–18, Sat./Sun.
10–20, Tel: 254 86 900
Museum for Communication
Leipziger Strasse 16, Tues.–Fr.
9–17, Sat./Sun. 11–19, Tel: 20 29 40
Palais am Festungsgraben
Am Festungsgraben 1, Wed.–Fr.
13–17, Sat. 13–20, Sun. 11–17,
Tel: 208 40 00
St. Hedwig Cathedral
Bebelplatz, Mon.–Sat. 10–17,
Sun. 13–17, Tel: 203 48 10
Topography of Terror
Stresemannstrasse 110/entrance
Niederkirchnerstrasse, daily 10–18,
Tel: 25 48 67 03

Leisure

Deutsches Theater
Schumannstrasse 13,
Tel: 28 44 12 25
Komische Oper
Behrensstrasse 55-57,
Tel: 47 99 74 00
Kunstsalon
Unter den Linden 41, art to
experience and buy, sale of old

costumes from theatre stocks,
Tel: 20 45 02 03
Maxim-Gorki-Theater
Am Festungsgraben 2
Tel: 20 22 11 29
Schauspielhaus
Gendarmenmarkt 3-4
Open to the public daily 10–20,
evening concerts,
Tel: 203 09 21 01
Staatsoper (State Opera)
Unter den Linden 5-7
Tel: 208 28 61
Tempodrom
At Anhalter station, large arena,
small arena, liquidrom, restaurant,
rooftop terrace, Tel: 74 73 71 72
Palace of Tears
Friedrichstrasse/Reichstagsufer 17,
Konzerthalle, Tel: 20 61 00 11

Festivals

Berlinale Film Festival always in
February, theatre festival always in
May, Carnival of Cultures always
at Whitsun, Christopher Street Day
always in June, Love Parade
always in July, Berlin Festival
Weeks always in September, jazz
festival always in early November

After eight

Cookies, Club
Charlottenstrasse 44/corner Unter
den Linden, Tues. and Thurs. from
23: cocktails, DJ
Barenger
US bar
Universitätsstrasse 2/3a, once a
week cocktails for half price,
Mon.–Thurs. 8–1, Fr./Sat. 8–2,
Sun. 10–1, www.barenger.com
Windhorst, bar
Dorotheenstrasse 65, Mon.–Fr.
from 18, Sat./Sun. from 21
Tel: 20 45 00 70
Emil, Schumannstrasse 15,
Mon.–Fr. 15–1, Sat. 17–1,
Tel: 559 74 54
BKA-Luftschloss, Schlossplatz
Discotheques, singles parties,
Tel: 251 01 12

ROUTE 2

Berlin

CENTRE WEST

From Brandenburger Tor to Tiergarten

HIGHLIGHTS

1 REICHSTAG
 Reichstag/federal parliament

2 CHANCELLERY
 Bundeskanzleramt

3 SCHLOSS BELLEVUE
 Bellevue Palace
 Hansaplatz

4 HOUSE OF CULTURES OF THE WORLD
 Haus der Kulturen der Welt

5 SIEGESSÄULE (TRIUMPHAL COLUMN)
 Grosser Stern
U Hansaplatz

6 POTSDAMER PLATZ
S **U** Potsdamer Platz

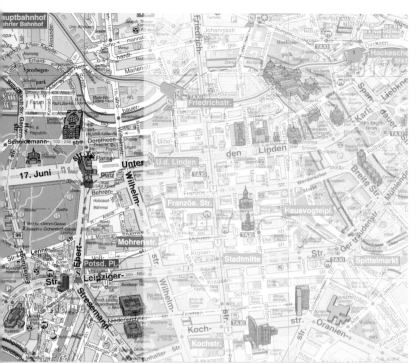

The green centre of Berlin extends from Brandenburger Tor to the Siegessäule (Triumphal Column) and from the Spree to Landwehr Canal.

It is the city's political, cultural and business centre.

PUBLIC TRANSPORT

Reichstag/federal parliament:
Bus TXL, 100, 248
Chancellery:
Bus TXL, 257
Bellevue Palace:
Bus 100, 187
House of Cultures of the World:
Bus 100
Grosser Stern:
Bus 100, 187, 341
Potsdamer Platz:
S 3, S 5, S 7, S 9, S 75, U 2
Hansaplatz:
U 9, Bus 341

Brandenburger Tor at the time of the Cold War between the Wall and cordoning-off barriers

Brandenburger Tor is framed by two squares, **Pariser Platz** on the east sick and **Platz des 18. März** on the west. Both names reflect political intentions: the eastern square, which had been just called "Karree" up to then, was given its name on September 14th 1814 and was intended to recall the victory over the Napoleonic foreign rule in the war of liberation in 1813–14, the entry of the allied armies into the French capital in late March 1814 and the Peace of Paris, concluded on May 30th 1814. The naming was less a homage to the French capital than a reference to the triumph of Prussia and its allies over France. The square Platz des 18. März to the west in front of Brandenburger Tor, on which Strasse des 17. Juni ends, recalls the gathering of the people of Berlin in front of the palace in 1848, at which they protested against the tyranny of the military. The highly cultured Friedrich Wilhelm IV ordered his soldiers to fire into the crowd and then fled very quickly

and secretly to Potsdam. On the evening of the same day, a hundred barricades were thrown up in the city centre; the March insurrections began and with them the revolution of 1848, which culminated in the National Meeting in the Paulskirche in Frankfurt.

Brandenburger Tor was also always a political place. Napoleon marched through it, as did Prussia´s regiments with Bismarck and

Brandenburger Tor in peaceful times: already an attraction

In the November nights of 1989, Brandenburger Tor was no longer merely a symbol, but again a gate to pass through.

Kaiser Wilhelm at their head and finally the columns of the SA on January 30th 1933.

For almost thirty years, Brandenburger Tor was a sandstone island in the no man's land between the two German states with curious people on both sides who couldn't see one another because they were separated by the Wall – which was three and a half metres high and three metres thick at this point. They were thus like the statue of that caller on the central reserve of the Strasse des 17. Juni: you see that he calls, but you can't hear him.

Here west of Brandenburger Tor President Ronald Reagan appealed to the Soviet leader Gorbachev to open the gate and tear down the Wall. And it eventually did come down. On the evening of November 9th 1989, the bulwark still resisted the rush of people from East and West Berlin, but two days before Christmas of the same year the gate was at last reopened in the presence of Chancellor Helmut Kohl, the GDR premier Hans Modrow, the governing mayor of Berlin, Walter Momper, and the official mayor of Berlin, Erhard Krack. Since then it has been open for everyone. In both directions. Day and night. But only pedestrians are entitled to pass through this place so steeped in history for the city and indeed the entire country.

A hundred years after its completion, the Reichstag was converted to accommodate the German federal parliament. Its original exterior (below, centre) was retained. In the interior, the general assembly (below, right) is now optimally illuminated by an avant-garde inverted cone (below).

The shortest way of describing the Reichstag building, which now accommodates the German federal parliament, would be "peripheral location with a view".

It is located outside the old and new centre of Berlin and with its main portal also turns away from the city centre. That's no coincidence: it was the will of the three emperors, under whose regency

the building was planned according to designs by Paul Wallot and built on the site of a former parade ground, popularly dubbed "Sahara" and at that time outside the city limits. The parliamentary system wasn't exactly dear to the heart of the emperors, who also insisted that the dome should be no higher than that of the Berlin cathedral, the court church.

Such considerations didn't have to apply for the latest conversion,

which was begun in 1995, immediately after Christo's shrouding of the building, and completed in 1999.

Sir Norman Foster set a dome – serving as chandelier towards the inside and lighting fixture towards the outside, ventilation duct and covered walk with lookout platform – on top of the building, which was left almost unchanged on the outside.

The people, to whom the building was already dedicated by Wallot, can either look down on their parliament or enjoy the unique city panorama.

The impressive **Chancellery**, whose park extends over the Spree to the other bank, is diagonally opposite the Reichstag.

This building, designed by Axel Schultes and built between 1997 and 2000, is the western part of a **"Federal Belt"** planned by Schultes, intended to consist in the axis of the Chancellery of the **Chambers of Deputies** – Paul Löbe House and Marie Elisabeth Lüders House – located at the eastern end and a citizens' forum between the Chancellery and the buildings for the parliamentarians. However, this project couldn't be realized due to lack of money. The new Chancellery with its 20,000 m² or so of usable space is thus rather enormous, but also rather lost in the expanse of the bend of the Spree.

The **Swiss Embassy** right next door – the only building here in the entire bend of the Spree that wasn't destroyed in the second world war – has, despite a very discreet annexe, thereby become even smaller and will in future be simply wedged in between the two monuments of the Chancellery and the **main station** that is to be created out of the former Lehrter station (incorporating high-rise buildings

in the glass roof). The two main victorious powers of the second world war, the USA and USSR, have left traces in the city landscape here, on the edge of the Tiergarten. The **Soviet Memorial**, built from the marble of the former Reich Chancellery, has stood on Strasse des 17. Juni since 1946.

Around the Chancellery: the Soviet Memorial (below), House of Cultures (centre) and new main station at the location of the former Lehrter station (right)

Chancellery, close to the Spree

The former congress hall, the present House of Cultures of the World, on the bank of the Spree half way between the Chancellery and Bellevue Palace, was donated to the city for the International Building Exhibition in 1956 by the US Benjamin Franklin Foundation.

The boldly designed roof collapsed in 1980 and was restored seven years later with a raised roof rim not using quite such avant-garde technology.

Bellevue Palace on the northern edge of the Tiergarten is rather like a spacious manor house. It was completed in 1785 according to plans by Michael Philipp Boumann as the first royal Prussian palace in classicist style and first served Prince August Ferdinand v. Preussen, the youngest brother of Frederick the Great, and later his son as summer seat. In 1843 it became crown property and then changed its purpose rather quickly before becoming Ethnology Museum in 1935 and Reich Guest House from 1938. It was badly damaged in the war, but restored both inside and outside in the late 1950s to serve as seat of the federal president. The palace itself always seems to be a little unused. Only the federal flag indicates whether the master of the house is present.

The new **Office of the Federal President** on an oval ground plan is only a few steps further on in the direction of the **Siegessäule**, almost hidden behind the trees. The smooth stones of the facade reflect the surrounding trees and give the impression that the building has always been here – at the back of Bismarck cast in bronze on a high pedestal, supervising the traffic am Grossen Stern, on which the Siegessäule (triumphal column) has stood since 1938.

The Siegessäule was originally installed in 1873 on the present Platz der Republik in front of the Reichstag to commemorate the German victories in the German-Danish and Franco-Prussian wars. It was moved in 1938 and at the same time raised with a drum in the column shaft, as it was in the way of the National Socialist planning for the Reich capital "Germania". Today, the monument, the "Goldelse", close on 70 metres high and topped by a Viktoria designed by Friedrich Drake, is one of Berlin's main sights – from below and from above, though you have to clamber up the spiral staircase with its 285 steps in the interior to enjoy the panoramic view from the platform at a height of 53 metres.

Bellevue Palace (below), seat of the federal president, on the edge of the Tiergarten. The Siegessäule (right) is in the middle of the Tiergarten.

The Tiergarten, a green oasis with artificial lakes in the middle of the metropolis, is fringed by the embassies of Mexico (right, above) and the Scandinavian countries (right, 2nd from top) and the Clarillon, Europe's largest Glockenspiel (right, below).

The Tiergarten, the giant park in the middle of the city, hasn't only recently been a people's park where the Berliners hold such enormous grill parties particularly in summer that generate so much smoke you might think the park is burning all over the place. But things were always pretty lively here.

This area, once richly stocked with game, served as a lordly hunting preserve from the 16th c. Friedrich II opened it up for the general public. In the 1830s the great gardener and landscape planner Peter Joseph Lenné created a landscape park satisfying both the requirements of the people and the court. Its basic plan still exists today. Numerous establishments were created on the edge of the park.

Memorial to the German Resistance in the courtyard of the Bendlerblock

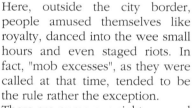

Here, outside the city border, people amused themselves like royalty, danced into the wee small hours and even staged riots. In fact, "mob excesses", as they were called at that time, tended to be the rule rather the exception.

There are numerous sights around this inner-city green lung (its effect is unfortunately reduced by the busy streets intersecting the park and on summer weekends it resembles a giant barbecue grill area): the **Academy of the Arts**, **Hanseviertel Quarter** (1956), Bauhaus Archive on Landwehr Canal, diplomatic quarter, **Bendlerblock with the Memorial to the German Resistance** and former Shell House on Reichpietschufer, very near the New National Gallery.

The **Cultural Forum** in the square between Stauffenbergstrasse, Tiergartenstrasse, Potsdamer Strasse and Reichpietschufer was created as a result of the appreciation in the late 1950s (and thus still before the Wall) that West Berlin, unlike the eastern part of the city, had no cultural centre. Hans Scharoun, architect and in the first post-war years also top city planner still for the whole of Berlin, advocated using the waste land between Potsdamer Platz and Landwehr Canal for such a centre. The area near the old city centre had been an administrative and exclusive residential area in the early 20th c. In the Third Reich, the plans of Albrecht Speer envisaged demolishing the entire quarter including the **Matthäikirche** to create an enormous "Runder Platz" ("Round Square"). Demolition work for "Gross Germania" began in 1938. Whatever hadn't yet been levelled here at the beginning of the second world war was destroyed during it, only the church and a few houses surviving, though seriously damaged.

Around these, the Cultural Forum with buildings initially all designed by Hans Scharoun was created

from 1960: the **Philharmonic Hall** (completed in 1963), whose external form is dictated by its inner layout, **State Library** (1976) diagonally opposite, which lacks any of the typical library mustiness, **State Institute for Musical Research and Musical Instruments Museum** (1984) at the Philharmonic Hall, **Arts and Crafts Museum** by Rolf Gutbrod (1985), **Chamber Music Hall** (1987), **Art Library** and **Collec-**

The Cultural Forum's most impressive buildings: the New National Gallery (left) by Mies van der Rohe and Philharmonic Hall (right) by Hans Scharoun

tion of Copper Engravings by Rolf Gutbrod (1993) and **Painting Gallery** (1997), into which Villa Parey, one of the few preserved buildings from before the war, is integrated. Next to this is the **New National Gallery** (1968) by Mies van der Rohe, a unique gallery that seems to hover on its just eight pillars and the architect's only building in Germany following his expulsion in 1938.

The Cultural Forum offers a cultural variety that can't be matched anywhere else in Berlin: five million volumes in the state library, over 600,000 prints, drawings and watercolours in the Collection of Copper Engravings, 750 exquisite musical instruments from all epochs in the Musical Instruments Museum, a really complete documentation of arts and crafts, from the Middle Ages to the present, in the Arts and Crafts Museum and an excellent, comprehensive overview of painting in Europe from the 13th to the 18th c. in the Painting Gallery.

To put the record straight so that no errors are made in the present about the past: **Potsdamer Platz**

The modern buildings of the Cultural Forum grouped around St. Matthäikirche (19th c.) include: the New National Gallery, Art Gallery, Painting Gallery, Collection of Copper Engravings, Arts and Crafts Museum, Philharmonic Hall, Musical Instruments Museum and State Library.

was never a square. It received its name in 1831 after Potsdam Gate was built by Karl Friedrich Schinkel at the western end of the neighbouring Leipziger Platz. But even then it was only a place where streets intersected, and in 1838 Potsdam station, the very first station in Berlin, was built.

But it is correct to say that in the 1920s the supposed square was the busiest place in Europe with trams, buses and cars converging from every direction. Three streets of houses intersected here as well as the underground from 1907. There was tremendous hustle and bustle in this business and amusement quarter. From 1945 the square was seemingly dead, and then, with the building of the Wall, dead as a doornail – nothing but a desolate, wide area. It has taken over ten years after reunification to awaken Potsdamer Platz back to a new, another life.

The Weinhaus Huth and Kaisersaal of the former Hotel "Esplanade", which has found a new location in the Sony-Center, have remained from history. The hall and wine house are memories of the past. Everything else here – the cinema, hotels, musical stage and casino – is present and future at one and the same time.

Potsdamer Platz, a traditional hub in a totally new guise. In the divided city, the square was border area and wasteland (left, above). The redevelopment, which has integrated the venerable Weinhaus Huth (left, 2nd from top), totally new arcades (left, 3rd from top) and the Sony-Center (left), extends as far as Landwehr Canal (right).

Adresses Centre West

Eating & drinking

Café am Neuen See
Lichtensteinallee 1
daily 10–23, Tel: 254 49 30
Facil
Potsdamer Strasse 3
Mon.–Fr. 12–15 and from 19,
Tel: 590 05 12 34
www.facil-berlin.de
Mediterranean cuisine
Joseph Roth Diele
Potsdamer Strasse 75, Mon.–Fr.
10–22, Tel: 26 36 98 84
www.joseph-roth-diele.de
Regular readings, inexpensive
cuisine
Paris-Moskau
Alt-Moabit 141,
daily 18–23.30, Tel: 394 20 81
Snackbar Spätzle, Bellevue S-Bahn
(city transit) station

Shopping

Potsdamer Platz Arcades
Alte Potsdamer Strasse 7
130 shops, boutiques and
restaurants on three floors
Mon.–Fr. 9.30–20, Sat.
9–16, Tel: 255 92 70
Royal China Manufactory (KPM)
Items for sale, Wegelystrasse 1
Tel: 39 00 92 15
Books and CDs, painting gallery
Matthäikirchplatz 8,
Tel: 20 90 55 55
Harb, delicatessen and wines from
the Lebanon
Potsdamer Strasse 93, Mon.–Fr.
9–13, Sat. 9–16, Tel: 265 16 27
Konditorei Buchwald
(confectioner's)
Bartningallee 29, layer cakes,
Mon–Sat. 9–18, Sun.
10–18, Tel: 391 59 31
Tiergarten flea market
Strasse des 17. Juni
Sat. and Sun. 10–17

Sights

Academy of Arts
Hanseatenweg 10, Tues.–Thurs.
10–19, Mon. 13–19,
Tel: 39 07 60, various exhibitions,
concerts, readings
Bauhaus Archive
Klingelhöferstrasse 14, Wed.–Mon.
10–17, Tel: 254 00 20, Mondays
admission free
Bendlerblock
Memorial to the German
Resistance
Stauffenbergstrasse 13–14,
Mon.–Fr. 9–18, Sat. and Sun. 9–13,
Tel: 26 99 50 00
Brandenburger Tor
Pariser Platz, daily 9.30–18
German Technology Museum
Trebbiner Strasse 10-15,
Tues.–Fr. 9–17.30, Sat. and Sun.
10–18, Tel: 25 48 40
Berlin Film Museum
Potsdamer Strasse 2, Tues.–Thurs.
10–18, Tel: 300 90 30
Painting gallery
Matthäikirchplatz 8, Tues.–Sun.
10–18, Tel: 20 90 55 55
Glockenturm (Black Tower), at
House of Cultures of the World,
bell concerts daily 12 and 18
House of Cultures of the World
John-Forster-Dulles-Allee 10,
Tel: 39 78 71 75
Art Library
Matthäikirchplatz 6
Exhibitions Tues.–Fr. 10–18, Sat.
and Sun. 11–18
library Mon. 14–20,
Tues.–Fr. 9–20, Tel: 20 90 55 55
Arts and Crafts Museum
Matthäikirchplatz
Tues.–Fr. 10–18, Sat. and Sun.
11–18, Tel: 20 90 55 55
Collection of Copper Engravings
Matthäikirchplatz 6

Adresses Centre West

Exhibitions Tues.–Fr. 10–18,
Sat. and Sun. 11–18
Studio gallery Tues.–Fr. 9–16,
Tel: 20 90 55 55
Lapidarium am Landwehrkanal
(stones)
Hallesches Ufer 78
for opening hours,
phone 43 09 53 33
Musical Instruments Museum
Tiergartenstrasse 1
Tues.–Fr. 9–17, Sat. and Sun.
10–17, Tel: 030-25481178
New National Gallery
Potsdamer Strasse 50
Tues.–Fr. 10–18, Sat. and Sun.
11–18, various exhibitions
Tel: 20 90 55 55
Reichstag building
Platz der Republik 1
Dome and roof terraces
daily 8–24
Last visitors admitted at 22
Rooftop restaurant daily 9–17 and
18.30–24
reservation under 22 62 99 33,
Visitor service of the German fe-
deral parliament
Platz der Republik 1
Tel: 030-22732152
Fax: 22 73 00 27
Bellevue Palace
Spreeweg 1
Seat of the federal president, not
open to the public
Siegessäule (Triumphal Column)
Grosser Stern, April–Oct. daily
9.30–18.30
Nov. to March daily
9.30–17.30
Soviet Monument
Strasse des 17. Juni
St. Matthäus-Kirche (church)
Matthäikirchplatz, Tues.–Sun.
12–18 and during mass

State Library
Potsdamer Strasse 33
Mon.–Fr. 9–21, Sat. 9–19,
Tel: 266 23 03
Leisure
Cinemaxx
Voxstrasse 4
17 cinemas
Regular screenings of films in
original language
Filmbar, daily 12.30–1.30
admission charged
Tel: 44 31 63 16
Imax
Marlene-Dietrich-Platz
Tel: 030-259290, large-format
vaulted cinema
Philharmonic Hall
Matthäikirchplatz 1,
for tickets phone 25 48 81 60
Stella-Musical-Theater
Marlene-Dietrich-Platz 1,
daily 17.30 and 20, admission
charged, Tel: 01805-54444
After eight
90 Grad, dance bar
Dennewitzstrasse 37,
Wed.–Sun. from 23, Tel: 262 89 84
Karakas Bar
Kurfürstenstrasse 9, Sun.–Thurs.
20–2 and longer, Fr. and Sat. 20–6,
Tel: 265 21 71
Spielbank Berlin (casino)
Marlene-Dietrich-Platz 1
daily 12–2, admission,
Tel: 25 59 90
Weinhaus Huth am Daimler-
Chrysler-Quartier
Potsdamer Platz
Restaurant and art gallery

ROUTE 3

Berlin

CENTRE IN THE WEST

From Charlottenburg Palace to Wittenbergplatz

1 CHARLOTTENBURG PALACE
U BUS Richard-Wagner-Platz

2 THEATER DES WESTENS
U BUS S Chancellery

3 KURFÜRSTENDAMM
U BUS Kurfürstendamm

4 BAHNHOF ZOO
U BUS S Zoo station

5 KAISER WILHELM MEMORIAL CHURCH
U BUS S Station Zoo

6 KADEWE
U BUS Wittenberg Platz

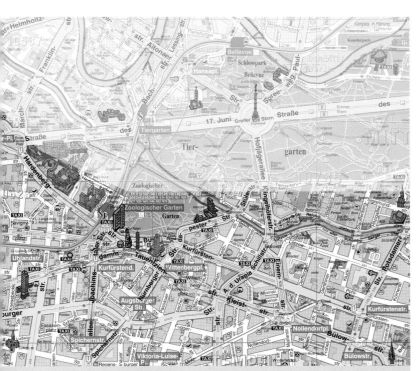

This was and is the centre in the west of Berlin: a long ribbon this side and the other side of the city transit line as far as Winterfeldplatz and Potsdamer Strasse.

PUBLIC TRANSPORT

Richard-Wagner-Platz:

U 7, Bus 145

Zoological Garten station:

S 3, S 5, S 7, S 9, S 75,

U 2, U 9, Bus X 9, X 10, X 34,
100, 109, 110, 145, 146, 149,
200, 204, 245, 249

Kurfürstendamm:

U 9, U 15,
Bus 109, 119, 129, 219, X 10

Wittenbergplatz:

U 1, U 2, U 15,
Bus 119, 129, 146, 219

Charlottenburg Palace, built in the late 17th c., is the most important preserved baroque monument in Berlin. The Belevedere in the park (left, below), monument of the Great Elector (below) and various sculptures in the park (right, below) all contribute to the beauty of the complex as a whole.

At the time **Charlottenburg Palace** was built, it was "jottweedee" ("Janz weit draussen", "far outside"), as the Berliners are still fond of putting it. Outside, but accessible in a direct way: from Brandenburger Tor westwards keeping straight ahead, via the Grosser Stern and Ernst-Reuter-

Platz, as far as the present underground station Sophie-Charlotte-Platz and then to the right into Schlossstrasse, a beautiful avenue lined with four rows of trees, leading direct to the palace courtyard.

On the left of the avenue, there is an interesting area of old buildings, created as a workers' estate at the end of the 19th and beginning of the 20th c. **Heinrich Zille** lived here, and you can still imagine the atmosphere he captured in his famous drawings.

The atmosphere of the palace is quite different. It was built in the last decade of the 17th c. as a **pleasure palace** for Electress

summer seat, was given its name after her death in 1705. The palace and palace park were a constant building site until the mid-19th c.: it was continuously added to and converted, supplemented and pulled down. Despite the very many architects employed here (Nehring, Eosander, Knobelsdorff, Langhans, Gentz and Schinkel) and the differences between the garden and landscape planners (Godeau, Eyerbeck and Lenné), a work was created over the decades that charms and continually surprises and, apart from the Armoury, is the most important **baroque complex** in Berlin.

Charlottenburg Palace was badly damaged in 1943 during the second world war, and there was much dithering after the end of the war as to whether the ruin should be demolished or the palace rebuilt. Restoration work then commenced in 1956 – but very gradually. In the interior, the restorers showed particular courage when replacing the destroyed ceiling paintings: instead of emulating the historic models, they simply applied the colour tones of the former paintings without any ornamentation or figures.

Sophie-Charlotte, commissioned by her husband Friedrich III, the later King Friedrich I. The building, which served the electress as

To take in and admire all the beauty and variety of **Charlottenburg Palace Park**, you would have to be able to look down on it: in the north, towards the city transit line, where it has the artistic naturalness of an **English landscape garden**, in which the sweepingly laid out paths intersect with picturesque river arms, small rises offer views and meadows between old trees are inviting places for relaxation. And in the south, towards the palace, where there is the strict geometry of a **French garden** with an octagonal fountain basin in the centre and side avenues of linden, offering shelter from sun, rain and snow.

The two gardens merge on the southern end of the carp pond. The **Belvedere** on the outer end of the park, which was once on a small island in the Spree and was used as tea house and lookout tower, is worth seeing in the garden, as is the mausoleum in the eastern park area, built as grave for Queen Luise between 1810 and 1812.

The **Mausoleum** contains the impressive cenotaph of Queen Luise and of King Friedrich Wilhelm III based on designs by Christian Daniel Rauch, as well as that of Kaiser Wilhelm I and Kaiserin Augusta, both works by Erdmann Encke.

The "New Pavilion" (1824–25) by Karl Friedrich Schinkel on a severely structured almost square

ground plan is east of the Knobelsdorff wing.

The palace complex includes the two **tower houses** of much more recent date to the right and left of Schlossstrasse. These were built in the mid-19th c. according to plans of Friedrich August Stüler as officer barracks of the Gardes du Corps. Both buildings were rebuilt in the late 1950s after having suffered serious damage in the war. The

Charlottenburg Palace Park, offering a stimulating blend of baroque garden and English landscape garden

eastern complex now accommodates the **Classical Museum** with the bust of Nofretete, the western the **Berggruen Collection**, presenting modern art with a special focus on the paintings of Pablo Picasso.

Charlottenburg Palace has in its immediate vicinity the Egyptian Museum with the head of Nofretete (far l.), the Berggruen Collection featuring numerous paintings by Picasso (2nd from l.) and the plaster moulding department of the State Museums (left).

45

Charlottenburg district, which has belonged to Berlin only since 1920, is divided in its northern part by the Foad leading straight as an arrow westwards from Schlossplatz in the district Mitte to Theodor-Heuss-Platz in the most affluent western part of the district. Today the street, which has in part eight lanes, is an important main thoroughfare in Berlin. It was created in its entire present length with the building of Charlottenburg Palace. In fine weather, an exciting view can be had from Theodor-Heuss-Platz, which is well above the level of the city centre because it is above the glacial valley, as far as the tower of the **Red Town Hall** in the city centre. To the right and left of this line, West Berlin presents itself in its entire variety – from the upper middle class quarters around Lietzensee, via the less well-to-do Wilmersdorferstrasse and the building of the Deutsche Oper, rebuilt at the end of the 1950s (up to then Theater des Westens served as opera house), past the generally closed **Schillertheater** to the oval **Ernst-Reuter-Platz**, marking the beginning of the university quarter with the **Technical University** and **University of Arts** stretching as far as Charlottenburger Tor (where there is a flea market at weekends) and the Zoo station.

Between Charlottenburg Palace and Zoo: Lietzensee (above, left) on Kaiserdamm, Deutsche Oper (above, right) on Bismarckstrasse, Theater des Westens on Kantstrasse and Ernst-Reuter-Platz (right) with the Technical University

Fast trip on the top deck

There are many ways of getting to know a city and gaining an impression of its size, sights and diversity.
If you're nimble and have lots of time, on foot you'll conquer a city strolling. On the other hand, if you haven't got any time, but lots of money, you can get driven around by a taxi in the hope that the driver doesn't just complain about the other drivers but also knows something about the city, although you shouldn't expect that from every "coachman".

The most authentic tours are still round trips of Berlin describing circles through the city of various distances and taking various times. You sit comfortably, obtain information in several world languages and then know that you've been almost everywhere. But it isn't quite as simple if you want to see again or even visit a place, a square or a house that has been leisurely passed by the city tours bus. That would presuppose well-nigh criminal flair.

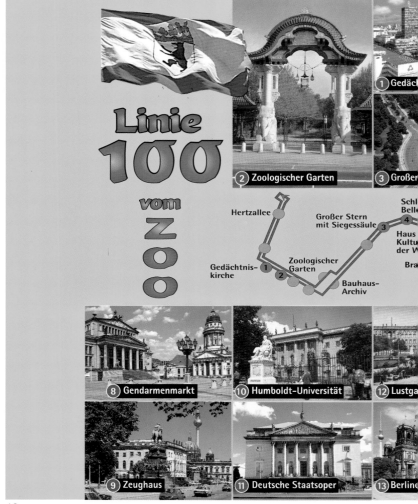

Linie 100 vom ZOO

① Gedäc[ht]

② Zoologischer Garten

③ Großer

Hertzallee

Großer Stern mit Siegessäule ③

Schl[oss] Bell[evue] ④

Haus [der] Kultu[r] der W[elt]

Gedächtnis-kirche ①

Zoologischer Garten ②

Bauhaus-Archiv

Bra[ndenburger]

⑧ Gendarmenmarkt

⑩ Humboldt-Universität

⑫ Lustga[rten]

⑨ Zeughaus

⑪ Deutsche Staatsoper

⑬ Berline[r]

A special form of seeing the city is offered in Berlin by public transport. The BVG, which runs the Berlin bus and underground lines, provides with the bus lines 100 and 200 what amounts to a quick view of the city centre area between Zoo station and Alexanderplatz. The double-decker of the line 100 BVG takes exactly 27 minutes to reach Alex from the station Zoo, while the 200 bus needs 26 minutes to reach the Zoo station from Alex. You need a normal ticket for 60 minutes though Berlin. If you'd like to take a more leisurely ride and keep on getting off, you can buy a day ticket and put together your very own programme.

If you take a bus, you'll also frequently be well entertained and informed by the drivers in the process. And not only in the first row above, though it still offers the best places.

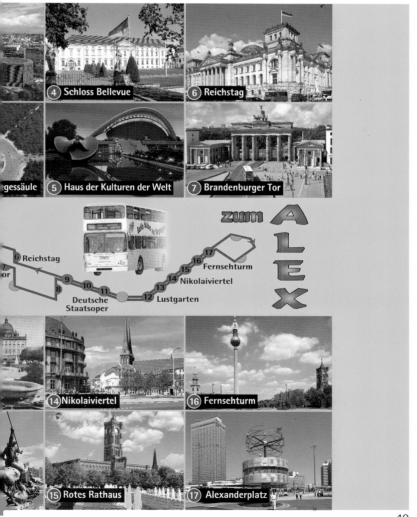

Zoo station, the main station of West Berlin until 1990

It's a very dubious privilege, but the significance of **Zoo station** for West Berlin when the city and country were divided can only really be appreciated by those who actually lived in one of the three west sectors at that time. All trains departed and arrived here at this only station for long-distance trains in the western part of the city. Many travellers arriving by train from cities with real stations thought they'd made a mistake: just two platforms with four tracks under the 16 metre high hall for long-distance trains wasn't even long enough to offer all travellers protection against the inclemency of the weather. The new arrivals

still didn't suspect that this unfriendliness of reception was made even worse by the tristesse of the poorly illuminated station hall. Anyone who arrived here wanted to get away fast, but not return immediately, as on the square in front of the station Berlin rather kept its word what with the hustle and bustle on the streets and in the two underground stations, neon signs, traffic lights, rushing and roaring traffic. Timid souls had every reason to start off fearing the city.

Today everything is different and better, lighter and also friendlier. The station will also be a stop for long-distance and regional trains in future, but there are other stations in the city as well. Today you can arrive in Berlin at many stations. The Zoo station, just like Friedrichstrasse station, the counterpart in what used to be East Berlin, is no longer a station of fate with a special significance that the two

One entrance to the Zoological Gardens is through the Elephant Gate at Budapester Strasse.

stations acquired only as a result of the division of the country and the city.

Up to late autumn 1989, there was probably nowhere in Berlin where people wept so much in public and together as on and in front of these two stations – the building at the station Friedrichstrasse is still called "Palace of Tears", where inspections of papers and faces and sometimes also body searches used to be carried out with very German thoroughness.

The station is certainly worth recalling. The city landscape around it has changed at lightning speed. The centre in the west has fallen behind compared with the old and new centre in Berlin Mitte. At the famous **intersection of Kudamm with Joachimsthalter Strasse** scarcely anything has remained what it was five years ago. The new houses are higher and more glamorous, the department stores have other facades, quite a few West Berlin institutions, such as Café Möhring, have disappeared or severely shrunk, such as Café Kranzler, and the Marble House is no longer any cinema, the Freie Volksbühne in Schaperstrasse only still occasionally a theatre, and you can also now again stroll with children through Augsburger Strasse.

The attraction that gave the station here its name – the **Zoological Gardens** along with its **Aquarium** – doesn't have to be reinvented. With its 34 ha, it is Berlin's second Zoological Gardens along with **Tierpark Friedrichsfelde**, which has fewer animals and fewer species, but is almost five times larger in terms of area. It was the first of its kind in Germany when it was founded in 1844 at the initiative of the zoologist Martin Lichtenstein and Alexander von Humboldt. The first animals were provided by Friedrich Wilhelm IV.

The intersection of Kudamm and Joachimsthaler Strasse, the centre of the shopping streets in the vicinity

Breitscheid Square with Kaiser Wilhelm Memorial Church and Europa-Center

When **Breitscheid-Platz** was still called Auguste-Viktoria-Platz, the world also wasn't perfect, but the houses around the square, on which there was only **Kaiser Wilhelm Memorial Church**, were intact. Today Breitscheid-Platz, named in 1947 after the SPD Reichstag MP Rudolf Breitscheid, who died in Buchenwald concentration camp in 1944, is an invention of the post-war period. Gone are the exhibition halls at the Zoo along Budapester Strasse and Romanisches Haus with the legendary "Romanisches Café" – **Europa-Center** is at its place today – and most of the original Kaiser Wilhelm Memorial Church, built here between 1891 and 1895, although it had actually been planned by the architect Franz Schwechten for Wittenbergplatz, has also gone.

This church, whose spire used to be 113 metres high, was badly

Mosaics from the end of the 19th c. preserved in the memorial hall in the ruin of the Kaiser Wilhelm Memorial Church

by the architect Egon Eiermann, who erected new sacred buildings including the 63 metre high ruined spire. Perhaps also because of the dispute concerning this new building, the church quickly became a symbol of West Berlin and the square a new centre, not least thanks to the Europa-Center, which was built at the beginning of the 1960s and with its 22 floors and height of 86 metres – the revolving Mercedes star on the roof measures 14 metres across – was already regarded as a high-rise building.

With its businesses, cafés, restaurants, cinemas and cabarets, the Europa-Center was a guarantee of life, a constant coming and going. Breitscheid-Platz first became an attractive square with the installation of the **Globe Fountain** by Joachim Schmettau in 1983 and the link thereby created between Europa-Center and Breitscheid-Platz – as it is free of traffic and, particularly on warmer days, a playground for all and sundry: beer drinkers and break dancers, dealers with and without tray, Kudamm strollers and Tauentzien saunterers.

damaged in the war. In the mid-1950s, there was a controversial debate about the future of the square – should it be demolished, rebuilt or kept as it was? The architectural competition was won

The elaborate and fanciful fountain installation on Breitscheid-Platz

Wittenbergplatz marks the end of the old centre of West Berlin with the Department Store of the West, or KaDeWe for short.

Here at **Wittenbergplatz**, at the east end of **Tauentzienstrasse**, the former classy western part of Berlin ends with what is very much the city's temple of consumption: the "Department Store of the West", or KaDeWe for short in German. Now department stores are generally scarcely mentioned in travel guides unless they happen to be particularly large and luxurious, such as Harrod's in London, or boast a splendid interior architecture, such as Galeries Lafayette in Paris. **KaDeWe**, opened in 1907 at the edge of the 200 x 140 metre square, has something of both: handsome interior design, an extravagant range of goods extending to the various luxury classes and above all – on the famous 6th floor – a food department with a wealth of things to buy that's really unique in Europe. Here you can find what you can't get anywhere else, and if you really don't get anything, you must have erred. The 7th floor with its restaurant conservatory is also worth seeing. The window seats are in great demand, and with good reason, as they offer a view over the city and Wittenbergplatz, which has in its centre the underground station Wittenbergplatz on an oval island. This was built between 1910 and 1913 and was very carefully restored in recent years. Three underground lines stop at it.

The absolute highlight in KaDeWe on the 6th floor: a food department catering to every taste

Wittenbergplatz has had its name since November 27th 1864, as has **Nollendorf-Platz**, one more underground station further on in an easterly direction.

That is no coincidence, as both squares were created according to the so-called Hobrecht Plan of 1862, a "development plan for Berlin and Charlottenburg", named after the government architect James Hobrecht, who envisaged a gridlike network of streets up to 53 metre wide for the still undeveloped areas, thus creating the basis for the city's open and very light structure.

Winterfeldplatz is in the middle of a quarter with numerous cafés, pubs and bars, with second-hand bookshops and little shops selling everything imaginable south of Nollendorf-Platz, which Berliners shorten to "Nolle".

Every Saturday a large weekly market is held on this square itself with simply countless stands and a very wide range of items on offer, from would you believe hand-harvested potatoes to self-woven linen to long-keeping sausages from Provence that are highly delicate in both taste and price. The throng at the market spills over into the cafés lining the square.

Still West Berlin's shopping street: Tauentzien between Kaiser Wilhelm Memorial Church and Wittenberg-platz

Addresses Centre in the West

Eating & drinking

Du Pont
Budapester Strasse 1, Haute Cuisine
Mon–Fr. 12–15 and 18–23, Sat.
18–23, Tel: 261 88 11

Harlekin in Grand Hotel Esplanade
Lützowufer 15, Tues. –Sat. 16–24
Tel: 25 47 80

Kaisersaal
Bellevuestrasse 1, haute cuisine
daily 19–24, cuisine until 23
Tel: 25 75 14 54

Le Canard
Knesebeckstrasse 88, Mon.–Sat.
from 12, Sun. from 17, French
cuisine, Tel: 312 26 45

Lutter & Wegner seit 1811
Schlüterstrasse 55, daily 18–2,
Tel: 88 13 44

Montevideo
Victoria-Luise-Platz 6, Mon.–Sat. 8–1,
Sun. and public holidays 9–1,
Tel: 213 10 20

Risto Vinoteca Cristallo
Knesebeckstrasse 3, Mon.–Sat.
12–24, Sun. 17–24, Tel: 312 61 17

Schell
Knesebeckstrasse 22
daily 12–1, Tel: 312 83 10

Tai-Tung with Hongkong Club
Budapester Strasse 50
daily 12–24, set lunch 12–16,
Tel: 261 30 91

Zwiebelfisch
Savignyplatz 7-8, Tel: 312 73 63
daily 12–6

Shopping

Arminiushalle
Arminiusstrasse/Jonasstrasse/Bugen-
hagenstrasse, stands, Mon.–Fr.
7.30–18, Sat. –14

Bad&Baden
Uhlandstrasse 54-55, Mon.–Fr.
10–20, Sat. 10–16, Tel: 883 91 00

Bramigk
Savignypassage/city transit arch 598,
knitwear for every day, Mon–Fr.
11–18.30, Sat. 11–16, Tel: 313 51 25

e27
Lützowufer 12, home living and
design, Tel: 26 48 02 70

H2O – The Water Shop
Bleibtreustrasse 3, tap water,
filters, specialist advice, Mon – Fr.

10–18.30, Sat. 10–14, Tel: 31 50 68 90

**Department Store of the West
(KaDeWe)** Tauentzienstrasse 21-24,
Mon.–Fr. 10–20, Sat. 10–16, market
am Winterfeldtplatz, every Saturday
morning

**Prinz-Eisenherz-Buchladen
(bookshop)**
Bleibtreustrasse 52, Mon.–Fr. 10–19,
Sat. 10–16, Tel: 313 99 36

Roadworx
Motzstrasse 9, skates and snowboards
Mon.–Fr. 11–19.30, Sat. 10.30–16,
Tel: 21 75 20 05

Rogacki
Wilmersdorferstrasse 145,
delicatessen, Mon.–Wed. 9–18
Thurs. 9–19, Fr. 8–19, Sat. 8–15
Tel: 343 82 50, www.rogacki.de

Stilwerk
Department store for designer
goods, Kantstrasse 17, Mon.–Fr.
10–20, Sat. 10–16, Tel: 31 51 50

Treykorn
Savignyplatz 13, jewellery, Mon.–Fr.
11–19, Sat. 11–16, Tel: 31 80 23 54

Sights

Collection of plaster casts of classical sculptures, Schlossstrasse 69b,
Thurs.–Sun. 14–17, Tel: 342 40 54

Egyptian Museum
Schlossstrasse 70, Tues.–Sun. 10–18,
admission charged, Tel: 34 35 73 11

Bröhahn Museum
Schlossstrasse 1a, Thurs.–Sun.
10–18, Tel: 32 60 06 00

Plaster moulding department of the
State Museums of Berlin
Sophie-Charlotte-Strasse 17/18
Mon.–Fr. 9–16, Wed. –18
Tel: 32 67 69-0

Heimatmuseum Charlottenburg-Wil-
mersdorf, Schlossstrasse 69
Tues.–Fr. 10–17, Sun. 11–17
Tel: 90 29 13 201

Kaiser Wilhelm Memorial Church
Breitscheidplatz, daily 9–19, memorial hall Mon. –Sat. 10–16 service
Sun. 10 and 18, admission free,
guided tours by agreement

Käthe Kollwitz Museum Berlin
Fasanenstrasse 24, Wed.–Mon. and
public holidays 11–18, Tel: 882 52 10

Kunstforum in der Grundkreditbank (art)
Budapester Strasse 35, Tues.–Sun. 10–18, Tel: 26 98 16 77
Mausoleum in Charlottenburg Palace Park, Tues.–Fr. 10 –12, Sat. and Sun. 12–17, Tel: 32 09 12
Museum for Early and Prehistory in Charlottenburg Palace (Langhansbau), Tues.–Fr. 10–17, Sat. and Sun. 11–17 Tel: 32 67 48 11
New pavilion in Charlottenburg Palace Park, Tues.–Sun. 10–17 Tel: 32 09 12 12
Berggruen Collection
Schlossstrasse 1, Tues.–Fr. 10–18, Sat. and Sun. 11–18, admission 1st Sun. in month free, Tel: 32 69 58 0
Charlottenburg Palace
Spandauer Damm, Old Palace: Tues.–Fr. 9–17, Sat./Sun. 10–17, New Wing: Tues.–Fr. 10–18, Sat. and Sun. 11–18, Schinkel Pavilion Tues. – Sun. 10–17, Belevedere April–Oct. Tues.–Sun. 10–17, Tel: 32 09 11 Charlottenburg Palace Park open until 20
Large Orangery in Charlottenburg Palace, Tues. and Wed., Fr.–Sun. 10–18, Thurs. 10–22
Tel: 326 59 94, www.spsg.de
Story of Berlin, exhibition
Kurfüstendamm 207/208, daily 10–20, Tel: 88 72 01 00
Verborgenes Museum – documentation of art by women
Schlüterstrasse 70, various exhibitions, Tel: 313 36 56

Leisure

America House
Hardenbergstrasse 22-24, Tel: 31 10 73
Camera Work, photo gallery
Kantstrasse 149, Tues.–Fr. 11–18, Sat. 11–16, Tel: 3150 47 83, www.camerwork.de
Deutsche Oper
Bismarckstrasse 34-37, Tel: 343 84 01
Europa-Center
Tauentzienstrasse 9, daily 9–24, shops 10–20
Tel: 348 00 88, www.24EC.de
Galerie Springer & Winckler, contemporary art
Fasanenstrasse 13, Tues.–Fr. 10–13 and 14.30–19, Sat. 11–15, Tel: 315 72 20,

www.springer-winckler.de
Komödie am Kurfürstendamm
Kurfürstendamm 206
Tel: 88 59 11 22, www.komoedie-am-kurfuerstendamm.de
Ludwig Erhard House
Fasanenstrasse 83-85, exchange daily 9–20, house 7–19
Tel: 72 39 01 58
Technical University
Strasse des 17. Juni, Mon–Fr. 8–20
Theater des Westens
Musicaltheater, Kantstrasse 12 Tues.–Sat. 20, Sun. 18, admission charged, Tel: 01 80-5 99 89 99
Wintergarten, Varieté
Potsdamer Strasse 96, Mon.–Fr. 20 Sat. 18 and 22, Sun. 18
Tel: 25 00 88 88
Zille-Hof
Old Berlin flea market, Mon.–Fr. 10–18, Sat. 10–16
Zoological Gardens
Hardenbergplatz 8 and Budapester Strasse 34, Nov.– Feb. daily 9–17, March daily 9–17.30
Apr.-Sept. daily 9–18.30, Oct. daily 9–18, aquarium daily 9–18, admission charged, Tel: 25 40 10
www.zoo-berlin.de

After 8

Bar jeder Vernunft, Kabarett in Spiegelzelt (cabaret)
Schaperstrasse 24, daily 19, admission charged, Tel: 883 15 82
Café Wellenstein, Viennese coffee house
Kürfürstendamm 190, daily 9–1
Tel: 881 78 50
Café Wintergarten in Literaturhaus
Fasanenstrasse 23, daily 9.30–1, Tel: 882 54 14
Kumpelnest 3000
Lützowstrasse 23, Sun. 17–5 Fr. and Sat. from 17, Tel: 261 69 18
Paris-Bar
Kantstrasse 152, daily 12–2
Tel: 313 80 52
Quasimodo Café
Kantstrasse 12a
jazz club, daily from 17, cuisine until 24, Tel: 312 80 86
Trompete
Lützowplatz 9, Sun.–Wed. 21–3, Thurs. 19–3, Fr. and Sat. from 22, bar, Tel: 23 00 47 94

ROUTE 4

Berlin

CENTRE NORTH

From Friedrichstadt-Palace to Scheunen Quarter

1 DEUTSCHES THEATER
`Tram` `U` Oranienburger Tor

2 FRIEDRICHSTADT PALACE
`Tram` `U` Oranienburger Tor

3 TACHELES
`Tram` `U` Oranienburger Tor

4 SYNAGOGUE
`Tram` `S` Oranienburger Str.

5 HACKESCHE HÖFE
`Tram` `S` Hackescher Markt

6 VOLKSBÜHNE
`Tram` `U` `BUS` Rosa-Luxemburg-Platz

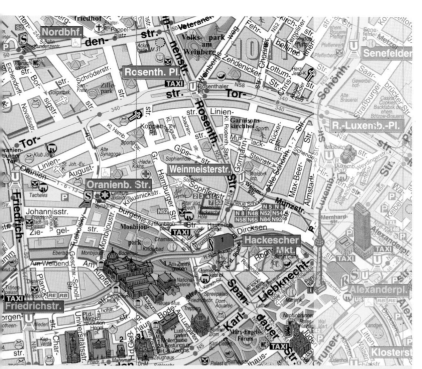

There is a very lively and diverse – cultural, scientific, business and entertainment – scene between the city transit line, Torstrasse and Hackescher Markt.

PUBLIC TRANSPORT

Oranienburger Tor:

U 6, Tram 1, 13, 50

Oranienburger Strasse:

S1, S 2, S 5, S 26,

Tram 1, 6, 13

Hackescher Markt:

S 3, S 5, S 7, S 9, S 75

Tram 2, 3, 4, 5, 15, 53

Rosa-Luxemburg-Platz:

U 2, Tram 1, 8, 15, Bus 340

North of Weidendammer Brücke, Brecht sits as a sculpture on Bertolt-Brecht-Platz (below right) and watches over the Berlin Ensemble. Diagonally opposite in Friedrichstadt Palace, the Revue Theatre comes into its own (above), while in Schumannstrasse top performmances are given in Deutsches Theater and the Kammerspiele (below l.).

Berlin theatre history was and is being written on the short stretch of **Friedrichstrasse** between **Weidendammer Bridge** and Johannisstrasse. West of Friedrichstrasse on the edge of the Bertolt-Brecht-Platz is the **Berliner Ensemble**, the stage founded by Brecht and Helene Weigel, which has had its venue here in the former theatre on Schiffbauerdamm since 1954. For decades it was the most prestigious theatre of the GDR internationally.

The former Friedrichstadt Palace – initially a despicable market hall, then a circus, finally a revue theater and a theatre seating 3,000 – is roughly on the present Brecht-Platz. The circular building fell in disrepair and was closed down in 1980 before being eventually

pulled down. The new **Friedrichstadt Palace**, a large theatre seating 1,900, a small one with

240, was opened in 1984 and is meanwhile the only establishment to continue the tradition of Berlin variety shows.

Deutsches Theater and **Kammerspiele** in Schumannstrasse, half way between Friedrichstadt Palace and Charité, are no less important for the history of theatre in Berlin. Both stages, accommodated in neighbouring buildings, are known well beyond Berlin, not least thanks to their prestigious managers and producers – Reinhardt, Hilpert, Langhoff, Brecht, Mann – who worked here and also made theatre history.

The Natural History Museum (above) is certainly as enormous as the dinosaur skeleton on display. This institution, which has no fewer than 60 million items, is connected with Humboldt University, as is the oldest hospital in Berlin, the Charité, which takes up the space of a small town (right, above). The former Hamburger Station (right, centre), which now serves as a museum for various exhibitions, is north of Invalidenstrasse.

The oldest and most traditional hospital in Berlin, the **Charité**, which is at the same time also Germany's oldest medical school, stretches down both sides of Luisenstrasse west of **Dorotheenstädtischer Friedhof** on Chausseestrasse, where many famous persons from German intellectual life have their final resting places. Originating from a plague house built in 1710 in front of the Neues Tor outside the city wall, the build-

ing became a garrison and citizens' hospital in 1726 and was given its name, meaning "Charity", by the soldier king Friedrich Wilhelm I in 1727. The complex was expanded in the 19th c. Only the smallpox hospital (1836) has remained from this time. The 21-storey high-rise building with a surgical centre was built between 1975 and 1985.

The Charité also includes the **Museum or Pathology** going back to Virchow Rudolf. Its collection of

once 23,000 items was decimated in the war, but is now again accessible to the public.

The **Natural History Museum** in Invalidenstrasse, which with its 60 million items is one of the world's six largest natural history museums, is part of Humboldt University.

The focus is on the dinosaur skeletons excavated between 1909 and 1913 in what is today Tanzania – including the world's largest brachiosaurus brancai specimen, 23 metres long and twelve metres high.

The mineralogical and palaeontological departments around the patio where the dinosaurs reside are no less important features of this museum, which was opened in 1889.

Two worlds, one of meditation, the other of fun very close together: the new synagogue with its gilded dome on the northern side of Oranienburger Strasse and the open-air swimming pool on the Spree in Monbijou Park on the opposite side of the street.

The former post office on the corner of Oranienburger/Tucholsky Strasse. Now used for exhibitions after having been empty for a long time.

Oranienburger Strasse begins at Friedrichstrasse with the Tacheles Cultural Centre in a former department store and ends at Hackescher Markt. But these few hundred metres are quite something. That isn't just because they offer a rare profusion of restaurants, pubs, cafés and bars next to one another, but also because this short stretch of street is nothing short of being a power pack of Berlin, rather subdued during the day, but downright wild and bold at night. It's been described as an agglomeration of "art and kitsch, failures and whores, Jews and the young". After German reunification, Oranienburger Strasse suddenly became the thoroughfare for prostitutes touting for custom – like a stage show of the oldest profession. That seemed to be new for quite a few, but did indeed have a very old tradition at this spot: Monbijou Palace, meanwhile disappeared, was built here in 1703 by Friedrich I for his mistress, Countess von Wartenberg, who is said to have begun her career in her father's sailors' pub.

But the quarter is also characterized by Jewish life: the **New Synagogue** with the Centrum Judaicum, the **Grosse Hamburger Strasse Memorial**, commemorating the Jews deported by the Germans to Auschwitz and murdered there, and also the **Jewish School**, which reopened in 1993.

Many of the secrets of this street are to be found in the courtyards and backyards of the houses. Here – such as in the **Heckmannsche Höfe** – galleries and boutiques have established themselves in an abundance and variety that you can't imagine on Oranienburger Strasse itself, through which the trams continue to thunder. You only have to dare to set foot in the courtyards.

Oranienburger Strasse narrows between Grosse Hamburger Strasse and Hackescher Markt. The houses here are also more modest.

Spandau Suburb began in the **Scheunen Quarter**. In 1672 the Great Elector Friedrich Wilhelm enacted a fire protection regulation decreeing, among other things, that 27 barns had to be built in front of the city wall east of Spandauer Tor in the area of the present Volksbühne at Rosa-Luxemburg-Platz so that easily combustible materials such as grain and straw could be stored outside the city. The area, which was then called Spandau Suburb, was swiftly developed and settled from 1700. In the 19th c., the Scheunen Quarter between the present Torstrasse and Münzstrasse as well as between Kleine Alexanderstrasse and Rosenthaler Strasse became a quarter for the have-nots, **"Berlin's back yard"**, which at the end of the 19th c. attracted increas-

The area north of Oranienburger Strasse features numerous courtyards such as the Gips-Höfe (below) through which you can pass from one street into the other. There is a garrison cemetery similar to a park in the north of the quarter, on Kleine Rosenthaler Strasse (below right).

Street cafés inviting visitors to sit and spend the time of day are to be found everywhere, as here on the corner of Tucholsky - Auguststrasse.

ing numbers of more or less destitute Jews fleeing from the pogroms in Poland and Russia. This was where accommodation was cheapest, and the residential district of old-established Jews around the New Synagogue was near at hand. During the Third Reich and the second world war, the people in this quarter were first deported and then the former structure destroyed. Today precious little remains of the former Scheunen Quarter. What you don't see you have to know: that, for instance, the **first cinema in Berlin** was opened in the house of the present Münz chemist's in Münzstrasse in 1899 and that

"Bergers Wiener Restaurant", run by an orthodox Jewish congregation, was in the 1st floor. Diagonally opposite, at the corner of Münz- and Almstadtstrasse, there used to be the notorious gangster pub "Münzglocke", in which the Christian underworld gathered, as in the "Mulackritze" in Mulackstrasse. The present Almstadtstrasse was called "Verlohrene Strasse" ("Lost Street") between 1700 and 1817. The old name was later terribly appropriate: the refugees from Eastern Europe didn't find a little piece of paradise here, as they had no doubt wanted, but stumbled into an anteroom to hell.

The northern square in front of the station at **Hackescher Markt** is just one big open-air café in summer. On less sunny days, of which there are more than plenty in Berlin, you can retire into the cafés under the city transit lines or look for a roof over your head in **Hackesche Höfe** and the neighbouring **Rosenhöfe**. At all these places, you can see much and be seen by many.

But this isn't the only reason for the great appeal of the area north of Hackescher Markt, which has constantly increased in recent years, thanks to a great extent to the courtyard complexes themselves.

Hackesche Höfe, named after Hans Christoph Friedrich Graf von Hacke, who was appointed military commander of Berlin by Friedrich II in 1749, is a unique complex of nine inner-city residential, event and industrial courtyards linked with one another on an area of 10,000 m². The complex, built in 1906, displays its entire splendour in its courtyards, which are decorated Jugendstil clinker facades partially glazed with colour. The neighbouring Rosenhöfe, opened at the end of 2002, are no less decorative

thanks to the architect Hinrich Baller's ornamental style.

Hackescher Markt as an event and shopping centre with its cabarets and variety shows, restaurants,

Restored to its former Jugendstil glory, the Hackesche Höfe complex at Hackescher Markt has become an attraction for locals and visitors alike.

The Volksbühne at Rosa-Luxemburg-Platz, today the most important theatre in Berlin with still incomparably low admission prices

cafés and bars, numerous boutiques and shops – always offering what happens to be particularly

hip – is extending northwards: via **Rosenthaler Strasse** in the direction of Rosenthaler Platz and via Neue and Alte Schönhauser Strasse towards **Rosa-Luxemburg-Platz**, on which the **Volksbühne** stands seemingly fixed and immoveable. It's the theatre in Berlin that presents the wildest and most courageous presentations of a top ensemble – at admission prices that again make going to the theatre an alternative to the cinema.

Centre North

Eating & drinking

Alcatraz
Neue Schönhauser Strasse 20
Upper-price category, cocktails and
snacks, daily 10–2, Tel: 27 59 67 20

Baccanali
Auguststrasse 36, Tuscan cuisine
daily 11–1, set lunch 12–16,
Tel: 30 87 20 94

Blaues Band
Alte Schönhauser Strasse 7/8
Vegetarian restaurant, daily 10–2,
cuisine served until 24
Tel: 28 38 50 99

Engelbrecht
Schiffbauerdamm 6/7, Mon.–Thurs.
Dinner for Two, Mon.–Sat. 18–1,
cuisine Mon.–Thurs. –23, Fr. and
Sat. –23.30, Tel: 859 85 85

Goa
Oranienburger Strasse 50, Far Ea-
stern cuisine, Sun.–Thurs. 10–2, Fr.
and Sat. from 10, cuisine,
Sun.–Thurs. –24, Fr. and Sat. –1,
Oriental Cocktail Lounge,
Tel: 28 59 84 51

**Cellar restaurant in Brecht House
Berlin**
Dishes à la Brecht and Weigel
summer daily from 12 (garden),
winter daily from 18, Tel: 282 38 43

Mare Be
Rosenenthaler Strasse 46-48
Mediterranean cuisine, daily 12–1
Tel: 283 65 45

Oren
Oranienburger Strasse 28,
Jewish cuisine, daily from 9,
Tel: 28 38 52 42

Matchmaker
Auguststrasse 91, French cuisine,
daily from 18, cuisine until 24,
Tel: 28 39 10 55

Sarah Wieners Speisezimmer
Chausseestrasse 8, Tel: 69 50 73 37

Schwarzenraben
Neue Schönhauser Strasse 13
Scene restaurant and pub, daily
10–2, Tel: 28 39 16 98

Vino e Libri
Torstrasse 99, Italian cuisine, books
and wines, daily 18–1,
Tel: 44 05 84 71

Shopping

Absinth-Depot
Weinmeisterstrasse 4, Mon. – Thurs.
19–24, Fr. 19–1, Sat. 16–1, Sun.
15–24, Tel: 281 67 81
www.erstesabsinthdepotberlin.de

Anna Chron
Torstrasse 93, second-hand furniture
classics of the 1960s and '70s,
Mon.–Fr. 14–20, Sat. 12–18
Tel: 44 04 65 14

Bonbonmacherei
Oranienburger Strasse 32, Wed.–Sat.
10–20, Tel: 44 05 52 43

Buttenheim Levi's Store
Neue Schönhauser Strasse 15
Jeans of yesterday and today,
Mon.–Fr. 12–20, Sat. 12–16
Tel: 59 44 60

Fishbelly
Sophienstrasse 7/ Hackesche Höfe
IV, Dessous, Mon.–Fr. 12.30–19,
Sat. 12–16

Katharina Sigwart
Oranienburger Strasse 27
Milliner's hats, Tues.–Sat. 12–20
Sun. Showroom 12–18
Tel: 28 38 45 95

Kostümhaus Jane Garber (outfitters)
Rosenthaler Strasse 40, Mon.–Wed.
11–18, Thurs. and Fr. 11–20 Sat.
11–16, Tel: 282 70 18

Lisa D.
Accessories, aprons, bags, Hackesche Höfe, Mon.–Fr. 11–18.30, Sat.
12–18, Tel: 282 90 61

Macchina Caffé
Alte Schönhauser Strasse 26
Espresso accessories, Mon.–Fr.
11–20, Sat. 11–16, Tel: 28 38 44 14

Quasi Moda
Rosenthaler Strasse 40/Hackesche
Höfe, Mon.–Fr. 11–19, Sat. 11–17,
Tel: 283 34 47

T 31
Atelier for jewellery
Tucholskystrasse 31, Mon.–Fr.
10–19, Sat. 10–16, Tel: 28 04 51 20

Trippen
Hackesche Höfe, shoes, Mon.–Fr.
12–19, Sat. 10–17, Tel: 28 39 13 37

Werkmeister
Friedrichstrasse 122, avant-garde
fashion, Wed.–Fr. 14–19, Sat. 13–16,
Tel: 44 04 27 90

Sights

Berlin Medical History Museum (Charité)
Schumannstrasse 20/21, Tues.–Sun. 10–17, Wed. –19, Tel: 450 53 61 22
Ott Weidt workshop for the blind (branch of Jewish Museum)
Rosenthaler Strasse 39, Mon.–Fr. 12–20, Sat./Sun. 11–20
Tel: 28 59 94 07
Brecht Weigel Memorial Chaussee-strasse 125, Tues.–Fr. 10–11.30, Thurs. 17–18.30, Sat. 9.30–13.30, Sun. 11–18, Tel: 283 05 70 44
Centrum Judaicum
Oranienburger Strasse 28/30, Sun.–Thurs. 10–18, Fr. 10–14
Tel: 880 28 300
Dorotheestädtischer Friedhof (cemetery)
Chausseestrasse, Galerie Wohn-maschine, Tucholskystrasse 35, Tues.–Sat. 11–18 Tel: 30 87 20 15
Hamburger station
Museum für Gegenwart, Invaliden-strasse 50/51, Tues.–Fr. 10–18, Thurs. –22, Sat. and Sun. 11–18, Tel: 20 90 55 55 www.smpk.de
Natural History Museum
Invalidenstrasse 43, Tues.–Sun. 9.30–17, Tel: 20 93 85 44
www.museum.hu-berlin.de
Neuer Berliner Kunstverein (art)
Chausseestrasse 128/129, Tues.–Fr. 12–18, Sat./Sun. 12–16,
Tel: 280 70 20
Postfuhramt (post office)
Oranienburger Strasse 35, various exhibitions, Tues., Wed. and Thurs. 12–22, Fr. and Sat. 12–22, Sun. 12–18, Tel: 85 73 01 27
www.berlinbiennale.de

Leisure

Berliner Ensemble
Bertolt-Brecht-Platz 1, box office Mon.–Sat. 8–18, Sun. 8–11
Tel: 282 31 60
Deutsches Theater/Kammerspiele
Schumannstrasse 13a, box office Mon-Sat. 11–18.30, Sun. and public hols. 15–18.30, Tel: 28 44 12 25,
www.deutsches-theater.berlin.net
Friedrichstadt Palace
Friedrichstrasse 107, Tues.–Fr. 20, Sat. 16 and 20, Sun. 16,
Tel: 25 00 25, www.friedrichstadtpa-last.de
Memorial for Divided Germany
Bernauer Strasse, Wall section and documentation centre
Grüner Salon in der Volksbühne
Rosa-Luxemburg-Platz 1
Tel: 24 06 58 07
Hackesches Hoftheater
Hackesche Höfe 1, performances from 20.30, Tel: 283 25 87
www.hackesches-hof-theater.de
Invalidenfriedhof (cemetery)
Zinnowitzer Strasse, parts of the Wall, watch towers
Die Distel cabaret
Friedrichstrasse 101, daily 20
Tel: 204 47 04
www.die-distel.berlin.de
Charité (hospital)
Schumannstrasse 20/21
Monbijoupark, daily, park restaurant
Roter Salon in Volksbühne
Rosa-Luxemburg-Platz 1, readings, dance, concerts, cabaret, from 18, Tel: 282 89 78
Volksbühne Mitte
Rosa-Luxemburg-Platz 1
Tel: 247 67 72

After eight

Mojito
City transit arches in Monbijoupark 157/158, Latin American cuisine, cocktails, daily from 12
Tel: 28 38 67 06
Bar-Celona
Hannoversche Strasse 2, every 2nd Thursday Flamenco, Latin American cuisine, Sun.–Wed. 12–1, Thurs.–Sat. 12–2, tapas until 1, Tel: 282 91 53
Bar Lounge 808
Oranienburger Strasse 42, Cocktail Bar, daily 10–3, Tel: 28 04 67 27
Tacheles
Oranienburger Strasse 54-56, café, cinema, events, exhibitions,
Tel: 282 61 85, www.tacheles.de
WMF
Ziegelstrasse 22, disco
Oxymeron
Rosenthaler Strasse 40/41, bar and restaurant, Tel: 28 39 18 86
Delicious Doughnuts
Rosenthaler Strasse 9, Club
Tel: 28 09 92 74
Ackerkeller
Ackerstrasse 12

ROUTE 5

Berlin

CENTRE EAST

From Schlossbrücke to Alexanderplatz

1 ALTES MUSEUM/
2 BERLIN CATHEDRAL

S Tram   Hackescher Markt

BUS   Lustgarten

3 MUSEUM ISLAND

S Tram   Hackescher Markt

BUS   Lustgarten

Tram   Am Kupfergraben

4 NIKOLAI QUARTER

U   Klosterstrasse

BUS   Mühlendammbrücke

5 MARIENKIRCHE

S Tram U BUS   Alexanderplatz

BUS   Spandauer Strasse

6 TV TOWER AT
ALEXANDERPLATZ

S Tram U BUS   Alexanderplatz

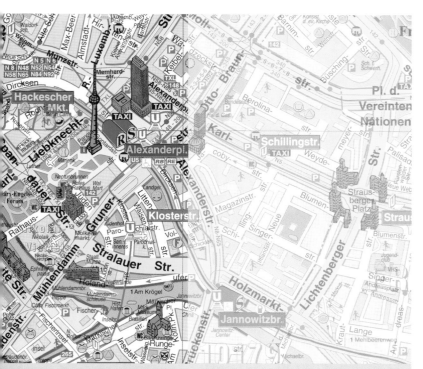

The city landscape between Kupfergraben and the TV tower features a green belt and the Museum Island, Nikolai Quarter and scattered remains of Berlin Palace.

PUBLIC TRANSPORT

Hackescher Markt:
S 3, S 5, S 7, S 9, S 75,
Tram 2, 3, 4, 5, 15, 53
Klosterstrasse: **U 2**
Mühlendammbrücke:
Bus 143, 148, 257
Alexanderplatz:
S 3, S 5, S 7, S 9, S 75,
U2, U 5, U 8, Tram 2, 3, 4, 5, 6
Bus 100, 143, 200, 348
Lustgarten: **Bus 100, 200, 348**
Am Kupfergraben: **Tram 1, 50**
Spandauer Strasse: **Bus 100, 142,**
143, 148, 200, Tram 2, 3, 4, 5, 6

Schlossbrücke, designed by Karl Friedrich Schinkel, linking Unter den Linden with the Museum Island

Nothing has remained of Berlin Palace, the former centre of the city and political power, after the ruin was blown up and the rubble buried at many places rather than disposed of or used for new projects.

The site shows few signs of once having been graced by a palace.

The **Schlossplatz** resembles a parking lot and a through street next to the former **Palace of the Republic**, now free of asbestos and completely "gutted".

There is the so-called pleasure garden facade of the city palace, integrated as reconstruction into the former **Council of State Building of the GDR** at Schlossplatz, because Karl Liebknecht proclaimed the republic and announced the revolution from the balcony of this portal on November 9th 1918 – on the same day and almost at the same hour Philipp Scheidemann did something similar from the Reichstag, without however demanding a revolution.

And there is finally the **Schlossbrücke** over the Kupfergraben, which was built in 1822–23 according to plans of Karl Fried-

Sculptures on Schlossbrücke, also based on designs by Karl Friedrich Schinkel

used to be a collecting point for the dogs for the royal hunt in the Tiergarten – had become necessary because the decrepit state of the old bridge didn't fit in at all with Prussia's new self-confidence after the wars of liberation.

Schinkel provided a design for a bridge decorated with sculptures, the government building commission worked out the construction costs, but the king approved only a stripped-down version. The sculptures were cancelled – the eight marble groups of figures, depicting the life of a hero from boyhood to death, were installed only between 1847 and 1857 and stood there for almost 100 years. They were removed in 1943 and put into storage after the end of the war in West Berlin. In 1981, on the 140th day of Schinkel's death, the West Berlin Senate exchanged the group of figures for the archive of the royal china manufactory with its 57,000 pieces as part of the first exchange of cultural artefacts between West and East Germany.

Friedrich Schinkel and with its historic parapet and eight monumental marble figures is one of Berlin's beautiful bridges. This new structure at the place of the former "Hundebrücke" – which owed its name to the fact that the bridge

Schlossbrücke in an historic illustration – with scarcely any traffic and no building sites

It certainly isn't all that common for a Protestant cathedral to be sited on the edge of a **pleasure garden**. But this is in fact the case here, on the northern part of the Spree island. It's not certain what was at this spot first. **Berlin Cathedral** is located at the site of the original church of the Dominican monastery of Cölln founded in 1297 at Schlossplatz. Its hall was combined with the palace chapel into a catheral chapter in the mid-16th c. At about the same time, Elector Johannn Georg created a fruit and vegetable garden on the marshy site that is regarded as the first **Botanical Gardens** of the city, but was left to grow wild in the Thirty Years' War. In the mid-17th c.,

Elector Friedrich Wilhelm had a pleasure garden created with a flower and vegetables garden as well as an orangery. Potatoes were also planted here for the first time in Berlin. At the end of the 17th and beginning of the 18th c., Friedrich I had the garden embellished with grottos, volaries, pleasure houses and waterworks and then opened it for all and sundry. Although there was already talk of a cathedral, the medieval church was first replaced by a baroque edifice before the present colossal neo-baroque building was built as mother church of Prussian Protestantism and as court and monumental church of the Hohenzollerns between 1893 and 1905.

The entree to the Museum Island is formed by the pleasure garden in front of the Altes Museum and the Berlin Cathedral (below), which served the Hohenzollerns as court church and as mausoleum. The present building, which was created in the transition from 19th c. to the 20th c. instead of other church buildings, has a surprisingly ornamental interior (right).

This building was 77 metres wide and 114 metres high up to the dome cross, accommodating 4,500 people in the dome area of the festival and sermon church.

The building was badly damaged in the war. In the course of the restoration begun in 1975, the dome and tower closures were reduced – the height up to the tip of the cross is now 98 metres – and the inner and outer structure a little simplified. Part of the mosaics, the magnificent neo-baroque pulpit and the Sauer organ have remained.

The pleasure garden in front of the cathedral is also again modelled on the design of Lenné from the 19th c. And the giant **granite bowl** is also back at its original place.

Altes Museum by Karl Friedrich Schinkel

The giant granite bowl in front of the **Altes Museum** with its diameter of seven metres, crafted between 1826 and 1829 by Gottlieb Christian Cantian out of a boulder from the Rauensche Berge near Fürstenwalde, as from its production to transport a masterly technical achievement of that time. It was actually intended for the dome rotunda in Altes Museum, but the statics of the building then didn't prove suitable for it. So it was installed in front of the Altes Museum – not to the detriment of this building, the prototype of a middle-class museum, designed by Karl Friedrich Schinkel.

This museum marks the beginning of the actual **Museum Island** with its five museum buildings: the **Altes Museum** (1824–28), **Neues Museum** (1843–46), **National Gallery** (1866–76), **Bode Museum** (1897–1904) and **Pergamon Museum** (1909–30).

The entire complex, which apart from the New Museum has been restored but is still sorely in need of renovation, accommodates unique art treasures of all categories – sculptures, paintings, archaeological findings – from antiquity up to the late 19th c. They were collected mostly during the late 19th c. after the founding of the German Empire in 1871 and there didn't prove to be sufficent space for them.

Unlike the buildings, the items exhibited and collected survived the second world war relatively unscathed: even at the beginning of the war in 1939 the museums here, like all other museums in the city, were closed and the collections packed and stored at what were considered to be safe locations.

Bode Museum, at the tip of the Museum Island

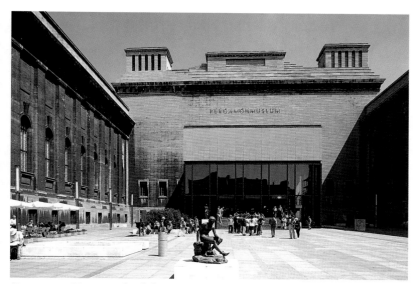

Pergamon Museum, built between 1909 and 1930

After the war, it was a long time before the treasures could be shown again in their original museums, as about 80 percent of the Museum Island buildings were destroyed.

The National Gallery was the first museum to open some halls in June 1949, and from 1950 parts of the Pergamon and Bode Museum were reopened, while reconstruction and restoration work on the Altes Museum took until 1982. The reconstruction of the Neues Museum began in 1985 and is still continuing, an important reason for this also being the fact that the financing of the maintenance and operation of the Museum Island remains uncertain.

Old National Gallery, a work by Friedrich August Stüler

The historic Nikolai Quarter was reconstructed during the GDR era. The Ephraim Palace (above), old fountain (below), Nikolaikirche, rebuilt in 1987 (far right) as well as the guest-house "Zum Nussbaum" (below, right) were integrated into the project.

The **Nikolai Quarter** between **Marx Engels Forum** and Mühlendamm on the one hand and the Spree and Spandauer Strasse on the other hand is a remarkable feat of city planning. The quarter already existed when there was still no Marx Engels Forum, no Spandauer Strasse, no Mühlendamm, but only the Spree as western boundary and in its vicinity the **Nikolaikirche**, mentioned for the first time in 1264.

This is the old town of Berlin, which was largely destroyed in the second world war and then demolished, apart from a few remnants.

A new residential quarter was built that was given the name Nikolai Quarter after the first church of Berlin, which was reconstructed at the same time on this site under the direction of the town planner Günter Stahn between 1979 and 1987. Apart from the church ruin as a medieval building, only the **Knoblauch House**, a residential house from the Gründerzeit (1871–73), a Jugendstil house in Poststrasse and buildings with several courtyards on the Spree bank were preserved. All the other buildings in this quarter are reconstructions on a grid defined by history.

Buildings that were of significance in Berlin but stood elsewhere were also integrated into the quarter. One is the guest-house **"Zum Nussbaum"**, which became famous thanks to its regulars Otto Nagel and Heinrich Zille, as well as a replica of the former court building from the 13th c.

Another is the 18th c. **Ephraim Palace**, a rococo jewel, on the corner Poststrasse/Mühlendamm, which has always stood at this street corner, but was completely cleared away with the widening of Mühlendamm in 1935 – and most certainly also because the owner was of Jewish faith. The 2,439 numbered facade parts of the house were stored in Wedding between 1935 and 1983. These were brought to East Berlin in 1983 following a decision by the West Berlin Chamber of Deputies. The corner house is regarded as the "most beautiful corner of Berlin".

The Spree bank of the Nikolai Quarter now boasts the larger-than-life monument of **Saint George as dragon slayer** by August Kiss, which was cast in 1855 in Lauchammer and was installed there in the first outer courtyard from 1856 until the palace was demolished.

Red Town Hall, seat of the Senate, the government of the city state of Berlin

The green area, now like a park, stretching from the Spree, from Marx Engels Forum eastwards, between Karl-Liebknecht and Rathausstrasse as far as the TV tower, was created after the destruction of the second world war. Before the war, this quarter was very built-up and oriented to the two buildings that still characterize the cityscape today here: the Protestant parish church **St. Marien** and the Berlin Town Hall, the so-called **"Red Town Hall"**, opposite.

The church dates from the time of the granting of a town charter to Berlin and Cölln and was probably begun between 1270 and 1280. The church, the second oldest in the city, was officially mentioned for the first time in 1292 and since then in fact continually converted, enlarged, extended and renovated.

It was given its present form in 1789–90 with tower superstructure with copper mountings according to plans by Carl Gotthard Langhans. The sacred building thus in itself a documents half a millennium of architectural history.

The entire history of Berlin from the beginnings up to the founding of the German Reich in 1871 is offered by the red town hall opposite, built between 1861 and 1869 on the site of the medieval Berlin town hall, which was probably built in the late 13th c. The historic court section of this house is in Babelsberg Park in Potsdam, a replica in the neighbouring Nikolai Quarter.

Around the town hall building of red brick – hence the name – there is below the 1st floor a terracotta fries running around the square

Marienkirche (above) dates from the early 14th c. – though not always in the same design. The Neptune Fountain (below) near the church was originally in front of the south side of the city palace, not being installed at its present location until 1969.

building, on which, beginning on the corner of Gustav-Böss and Jüdenstrasse, the history of Berlin is presented in more or less lively scenes.

The **Neptune Fountain**, originally installed on the southern square in front of the city palace, is now between the town hall and Marienkirche. In this vigorous work by Reinhold Begas (1891), a brawny Neptune thrones a massive rock amidst a maze of incessantly active water spouts.

The two gentlemen, who were installed in 1986 as sculptures in twice life size in the centre of **Marx Engels Forum** staring eastwards as if they were mummified, pale before so much water spouting.

"The square", Alfred Döblin wrote in 1928, "is no longer the same as it was the previous year." And at other place: "At Alexanderplatz they bungle and continue to bungle."

The World Time Clock on Alexanderplatz continues to be the place where people rendezvous if they don't want to miss one another.

The facade of the 10-storey block on the northern edge of **Alexanderplatz** – seat of the federal environment ministry – presents a quotation from Döblin's novel on its entire width and height as reference to the square's more recent history. It received its name in 1805, on the occasion of a Berlin visit by the zar Alexander I.

Previously it was called what it was, namely "Ochsenmarkt" (oxen market), because the cattle market was held here, and "Paradeplatz", because it served as parade ground.

Alexanderplatz gained its present form mainly with the expansion of the East Berlin city centre between 1966 and 1970. At that time, the

The fountain that gives Alexanderplatz city flair

Centrum department store was created, then the largest department store in the GDR and – connected with the department store via the "Alex-Passage" – the 123 metre high **Hotel "Stadt Berlin"** and to the north the 10-storey House of the Electrical Industry and the 17-storey **"House of Travel"**. The neighbouring **"House of the Teacher"** with the congress hall was already built between 1961 and 1964.

The decorative elements at that time on the 3 ha square, completely paved with concrete slabs, have remained: the **fountain** and the **World Time Clock**, both erected in 1969.

The highlight of the square standing since 1969 on the far side of the city transit line is the **TV tower**, 365 metres high, a glassed-in tower dome at a height of about 200 metres in which there is a café seating 200 mounted on one rotating ring. Anyone who has no idea of the size of Berlin at ground level gets it here above: an entire rotation of the café takes half an hour.

It is 365 metres from the futuristic base (below) to the tip of the TV tower (right). No building in Berlin is higher.

Addresses Centre North

Eating & drinking

Altes Museum cafeteria
Bodestrasse 1-3, Sun.–Fr. 9–17,
Sat. 9–20
Tel: 20 35 53 37

Azuma Sushi
Rathausstrasse 23, Mon.–Sat.
12–14 and 19–24
Tel: 247 83 53

Brauhaus Georgbräu
Spreeufer 4, in summer daily
10–24, in winter Mon.–Fr. from 12,
Tel: 242 42 44

Café Zsolnay
Hungarian cuisine, Hungarian culture, cinema, Mon.–Fr. 14–22, Sat.
and Sun. 12–22
Tel: 241 57 15

China Garden
Rathausstrasse 23, daily 12–24,
Tel: 247 83 56

Green's
Poststrasse 13, small café,
daily from 11
Tel: 24 72 60 40

Historic wine bars in Knoblauch
House, Nikolai Quarter
Poststrasse 23, daily 11–24,
in summer 11–1
Tel: 242 41 07

La Riva
Spreeufer 2, Italian cuisine,
daily 11–23

Mutter Hoppe
Rathausstrasse, daily 11.30–24,
Tel: 24720603

Podewil
Klosterstrasse 68-70, Italian cuisine,
daily 12–20 Tel: 242 67 45

Reinhards
Poststrasse 28, international
cuisine, daily 9–1, Tel: 238 42

Zum Nussbaum
Nikolai Quarter, German cuisine,
daily 12–2, Tel: 242 30 95

Zur letzten Instanz
Waisenstrasse 16, Mon.–Sat. 12–1,
Sun. 12–23

Shopping

Asia Mekong
In Alexanderhaus am Alexander-
platz, Asian specialities,
Mon.–Fr. 10–19, Sat. 10–16,
Tel: 559 36 41

Berlin Carré
Karl-Liebknecht-Strasse 13

Birkenparadies
Probststrasse 4, Nikolai Quarter,
Siberian woodcarvings
Tel: 24 72 65 49

Der Teeladen (tea)
Propststrasse 3, Nikolai Quarter
Tel: 242 32 55

Die Puppenstube
Propststrasse 4, Nikolai Quarter
Tel: 242 39 67

Karibische Zigarren (cigars)
Probststrasse 4, Mon.–Fr. 10–20

Kaufhof Galeria
Largest department store in East
Berlin, Alexanderplatz 9, Mon.–Fr.
9–18.30, Sat. 9–16
Tel: 24 74 30

Saturn
Alexanderplatz 8, multimedia market, Tel: 24 75 16

Thuringian Christmas market
Probststrasse 8, Nikolai Quarter
Tel: 241 12 29

Wohltat'sche Buchhandlung
(bookshop)
Alexanderplatz 2, Tel: 242 68 54

Sights

Old National Gallery
Museumsinsel, Bodestrasse 1-3,
Tues.–Sun. 10–18, Thurs. –22,
Tel: 20 90 55 55, www.smpk.de

Altes Museum
Bodestrasse 1-3, Tues.–Sun.
10–18, Thurs. –22,
Tel: 20 90 55 55, www.smpk.de

Classical Collection, Pergamon
Museum

art'otel Ermelerhaus
Wallstrasse 70-73, Tel: 24 06 20

Berliner Dom (Berlin Cathedral)
Am Lustgarten, daily 9–19
concerts and tours
Tel: 20 26 91 36
Bode Museum
Museum Island, Bodestrasse 1-3
Closed until 2005
Ephraim-Palais
Poststrasse 16, Tues.–Sat. 10–18,
Tel: 24 00 20
Fernsehturm (TV tower)
Alexanderplatz, March–Oct. daily
9–1, café 10–1, Nov.–Feb. daily
10–24, lookout platform
Knoblauch House
Poststrasse 23, Tues.–Sat. 10–18,
Tel: 24 00 20
St.-Marien church
Karl-Liebknecht-Strasse 8,
Mon.–Thurs. 10–16, Sat. and Sun.
12-16
Marx-Engels-Forum
between Karl-Liebknecht-Strasse
and Nikolai Quarter
Museum for Islamic Art >
Pergamon Museum
Nikolaikirche, Nikolaiplatz
Tues.–Sun. 10–18, Glockenspiel
10, 12, 14, 16 and 18
Tel: 24 72 45 29
www.stadtmuseum.de
Pergamonmuseum, Museum
Island Bodestrasse 1-3, Tues.–Sun.
10–18, Thurs.–22
Tel: 20 90 55 55, www.smpk.de
Rotes Rathaus (Red Town Hall)
Rathausstrasse 15, Mon–Fr. 9–18,
Tel: 90 260
Stadtgericht (court)
Littenstrasse 13–15,
Mon–Fr. 8–18
Near East Museum > Pergamon
Museum
Leisure
Podewil
Klosterstrasse 68-70, concerts,
events
Tel: 24 22 42 67 45
Spielcasino
Alexanderplatz, Tel: 23 80 77 00

ROUTE 6

Berlin

CENTRE OF THE SCENE

From Bernauer Strasse to Kreuzberg

1 MEMORIAL
BERNAUER STRASSE
 Nordbahnhof/
Gartenstrasse

2 KOLLWITZPLATZ
 Senefelder Platz

3 FRANKFURTER ALLEE
 Straussberger Platz

4 EAST-SIDE-GALLERY
5 OBERBAUMBRÜCKE
 Warschauer
Strasse

6 TREPTOWER PARK
 Treptower Park

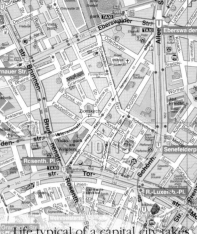

Life typical of a capital city takes place in the centre of Berlin and around the centre the real life. In some places it is wilder, more exciting and colourful.

PUBLIC TRANSPORT
Nordbahnhof/Gartenstrasse:
S 1, S 2, S 25, S 26, Bus 147, 245, Tram 8, 50
Senefelder Platz: **U 2, Bus 143**
Straussberger Platz: **U 5, Bus 142**
Warschauer Strasse: **S 6, S 8, S 9, Bus 142, Tram 23, U 1, U 12, U 15**
Treptower Park: **S 6, S 8, S 9, Bus 104, 166, 167, 194, 265**

Bernauer Strasse formed the boundary between the city districts Wedding and Mitte. After the building of the Wall, it thus became part of the border between East and West Berlin. The Berlin Wall Memorial is on the former border strip at the level of Ackerstrasse.

There are only a few places in the inner city area of Berlin at which even today the course of the former wall can be identified as precisely as here on the southern side of **Bernauer Strasse** from Nordbahnhof to Schwedter Strasse. A wide lane was cut here in the city landscape in 1965–66, the GDR demolishing the residential buildings as well as the back yards, which belonged to district Mitte and thus to East Berlin, to prevent any more East Germans trying to escape the regime by entering these houses and dropping down on the West Berlin pavement in front of the buildings.

At a memorial to the Wall and the people who died attempting to flee the East German regime, a **monument**, consisting of a memorial and an original section of the former border strip was erected in this lane in the area of Ackerstrasse.

The former "death zone" on the east end of Bernauer Strasse is used quite differently. Here the

Mauerpark, a park area with still rather paltry little trees, was created between **Ludwig-Jahn-Sportpark** and **Max-Schmeling Hall**. Particularly when the weather is warm, this is like a very lively

The Wall Park is so called because it is where the Wall actually ran west of Ludwig-Jahn-Sportplatz. Particularly in summer, the green area between Eberswalder- and Gleimstrasse is an amusement park in which the people ensure quite by themselves that they have a good time.

recreational park, in which visitors can and must organize their relaxation and fun as they fancy: no booths, no establishments of whatever shape or form, no programme is offered here. The Wall Park is a a completely new type of people's park. A revolution isn't one of them.

But this was certainly on the programme here on March 26th 1848. Here, on the present site of the Wall and sport park, there gathered on the then parade ground under the **"Einsame Pappel"** 20,000 workers and craftsmen, not to overthrow King Friedrich Wilhelm IV, but to promote work for everybody – workers, craftsmen, small entrepreneurs. The "lonely poplar" on the southeastern corner of the area has meanwhile become a poplar grove.

Zionskirchplatz, north of Rosenthaler Platz, a green oasis in the middle of the sea of houses with the Protestant Zion church (1866–73) in its centre

91

At the underground station Eberswalder Strasse three streets intersect under the overhead railway: here all ways lead to fun.

Today the intersection of Schönhauser Allee and Danziger Strasse and the street of houses Kastanien- and Pappelallee is nothing but the heart of **Prenzlauer Berg**. All the attractive quarters are very close to here: the Wall Park with **Oderberger Strasse**, **Helmholtzplatz** with its adjoining and side streets and **Kollwitzplatz**, which has a

playground in its centre and is all around a playground for adults.

Today all these quarters have a liveliness they didn't have originally. A start was made in the 1860s developing the previous village fields on the basis of the Hobrecht Plan. Work proceeded very fast, so that a closely settled workers' district was created in a few decades: over 350,000 people lived on less than ten square km here up to the end of the first world war.

Prenzlauer Berg belonged to "built-up Berlin": behind the dolled-up facades of the houses there were small and minute apartments, dark courtyards and backyards, with miserable hygienic conditions.

In the last ten years, an attractive quarter that is well worth visiting has been created between Kollwitzplatz with a sculpture of the artist (left) and the water tower at the southern end of Rykestrasse (right).

This structure of the district survived the Weimar Republic, National Socialism and the second world war. During the GDR era, it became the eastern counterpart of Kreuzberg in the west: a sizeable niche for nonconformists, dropouts and also rebels in an area that the state intentionally let run down. When the East Germans rose up against party rule, it was utterly natural that the centre of the conflicts in Berlin was in Prenzlauer Berg – the **Gethsemane Church** on Stargarder Strasse became the stronghold of this resistance and is today its symbol.

For the first weeks and months after the fall of the Wall, the district experienced a winter of anarchy and the area came to be regarded as the "hottest address in the whole of Central Europe".

That is a past that can also no longer be experienced. Prenzlauer Berg has developed from a poor people's quarter into one of the most attractive residential areas in the immediate neighbourhood of the eastern city centre.

Relics of the recent and not so recent past are the BFC stadium at the Wall Park, the occasionally open city baths in Oderberger Strasse, Berlin's most famous curry sausage snack bar under the overhead railway on Eberswalder Strasse (although the sign "Konopke" is still on it, the Konopkes are no longer there), the **Jewish cemetery** between Schönhauser Allee and Kollwitzstrasse with the renovated Judengang, the **synagogue** in Rykestrasse, the neighbouring **water tower** on the former Windmühlenberg and finally, rather invisible from below, the flat roof on the pointed residential building at the junction of Kastanienallee and Schönhauser Allee where above the Skladinowski brothers made their first, still very complex attempts with moving pictures, with film.

Thälmann Park with the monstrous statue of Thälmann (above), Friedrichshain People's Park with the Märchenbrunnen (right, centre), the Velodrom on Landsberger Allee (above, outside) and the dead-straight Karl-Marx-Allee leading to the east (below) are very diverse attractions on the periphery of the city centre.

How the GDR imagined residential quarters in modern times can be seen north of Danziger Strasse between the city transit stations Prenzlauer Allee and Greifswalder Strasse. The **Ernst Thälmann Park** here is opened towards Prenzlauer Allee with a **planetarium**, built in 1983– 87, and ends at Greifswalder Strasse with the more than life-size **bronze bust** of the former communist party chairman, designed by Lew Kerbel, on the forum-like square of marble and natural stone – the metal nose of the great chairman is heatable, as it wasn't considered desirable having snow on it in winter.

The Ernst Thälmann estate with 8-storey high-rise buildings and 12 – 18 storey tower blocks in large panel construction is on the edge of the park, created on the site of Berlin's oldest gas works, which was demolished in 1982.

Friedrichshain People's Park to the south was created between 1846 and 1848 and is the oldest park in the city centre after the Tiergarten. It was devastated during the second world war and afterwards redesigned using the rubble left over from the war. Since then it has also had the two hills.

Karl-Marx-Allee between Alexanderplatz and Frankfurter Tor is also built on a landscape of rubble. The blocks, very much oriented to the overelaborate decorated style of the USSR under Stalin along the 90 metre wide arterial road, have become what they were supposed to become: "palaces for the people".

Sightseeing by city transit (S-Bahn)

The most convenient and most exciting way of discovering the inner city is by taking the city transit. Since the ring around the inner city area has again been closed, you can circle around the city centre changing twice. That is inex-

pensive and offers the opportunity to take a look at the back of the city landscape. The route on the circle line, also called "dog's head" (the lines resemble the profile of a dog with floppy ears looking westwards), curvers through the entire

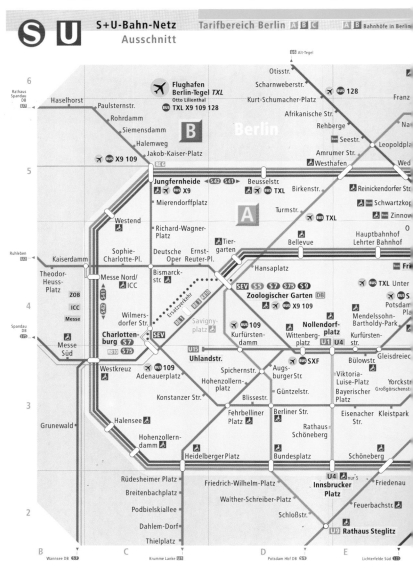

city area, offers quick glances into the rooms of the houses built near the tracks, opens up broad city areas that one never gets to see differently and on this trip round through Berlin also shows the differences between the districts. It's a trip through the city and its day-to-day life. It's difficult to decide whether to sit on the outside or inside of the carriage. Actually, it'd be best to take two round trips.

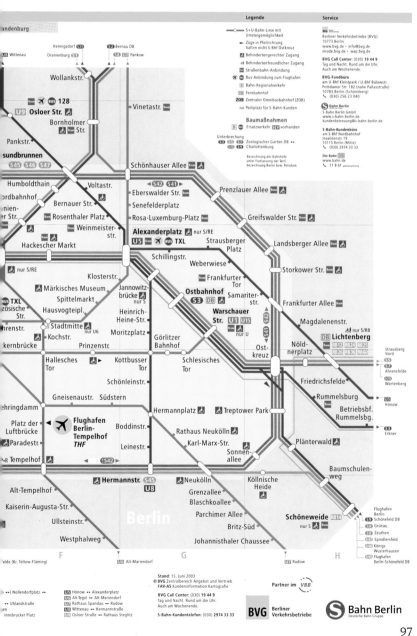

What Prenzlauer Berg stood for in the first years after reunification is now Friedrichshain – in any case the part between Frankfurter Allee in north, Spree in south, Warschauer Strasse in the west and Ringbahn in east. If civilized anarchy prevailed in Prenzlauer Berg, it's now civilised chaos around Wühlisch and Simon-Dach-Strasse. In the last few years simply countless restaurants of every type and bars to suit every taste have opened in the ground floors of not yet refurbished houses here. The apartments are cheap, the prices moderate, the parking space scarce, and the people still go a lot on foot.

This part of Friedrichshain is separated from Kreuzberg and Treptow only by the Spree. Along the border to Kreuzberg, which also used to be the border in divided Berlin, the East-Side-Gallery exhibits its multicoloured paintings on the concrete of the former Wall.

Treptow, which begins on the far side of the city transit ring, is with Treptow Park and the adjoining park also an enormous recreation facility. The centre still features the

traditional **Gasthaus "Zenner"**, which has been in this square since 1776.

It's often said to be the most beautiful view of Berlin: in the middle the Spree, to the right Friedrichshain, to the left Kreuzberg, linked by the Oberbaumbrücke and on the horizon the silhouette of the city centre.

In Treptow Park itself, a landscape park of the people's park movement of the 19th c., stands at the edge the Archenhold Observatory and in the centre, on the site of a former playground, the Soviet Memorial with a mausoleum, on which there is the giant bronze sculpture of a Soviet soldier holding a saved child.

The border used to run along Mühlenstrasse on the northern bank of the Spree. Today the painted Wall remnants are the "East-Side-Gallery" (left). Treptow Park features the huge Soviet Memorial honouring the feats of heroism and sacrifices of the Red Army soldiers during the second world war.

According to the latest survey of the state statistical office (mid-2001), 2,896,930 persons with and 436,182 persons without German citizenship live in Berlin. The highest share of persons of non-Germans is in the district Mitte ahead of the districts Friedrichshain-Kreuzberg and Neukölln. Close on half of all foreigners in Berlin live in these three districts. The former district **Kreuzberg**, now combined with Friedrichshain, has the longest tradition with a high share of foreigners of the population. In Kreuzberg, the former S0 36 (so-called after a postal delivery zone), the area around the underground stations Kottbusser Tor and Görlitzer station, has the highest share of foreigners. After the division of the city by the building of the Wall, Kreuzberg became a peripheral area. Anyone who could afford it moved to "better" areas. The underprivileged remained and foreigners came, as well as students, artists and people on the lookout for alternative forms of living. This mixture, hitherto unknown in Germany, was initially highly explosive, later obstreperous and self-confident,

The "Estrel", the largest hotel in Germany (above), is located in Neukölln in the transition to the neighbouring district Treptow. Görlitzer Park (below) is one of the few parks in the densely built-up part of Kreuzberg, which used to be called "SO 36".

A giant market is held every Tuesday and Friday on the Maybach bank along Landwehr Canal, catering largely to the requirements of the local Turks.

today composed. The people live and talk with one another, shop at the same places, gather on **Mariannenplatz** in front of Bethanien in summer and in Turkish tea rooms and German pubs in winter. Nowhere else in Berlin is there such a variety with respect for differences, nowhere else are there so many cultural associations, theatre groups, cinema, variety shows and music stages, nowhere else is there almost continuously so much life on the streets. SO 36 is in – though already for a rather long time.

In SO 36 from Moritzplatz east of Oranienstrasse it isn't German or Turkish either – it's both at the same time.

The gymnastics founder Jahn, who practised his gymnastic exercises in Hasenheide in Neukölln, was rewarded with a monument.

SO 36 is bordered to the south by **Hasenheide** between the street of the same name and Columbia-damm. The use of the area as an enclosure for hares going back to 1678 gave the park its name. Here in 1811 **Friedrich Ludwig Jahn** taught for the first time German men in German physical training and was rewarded with a monument. In Jahn's day, the later park was still a military training ground. From 1838 it was designed as a landscape garden by Peter Joseph Lenné and constantly scaled down up to 1939, especially with the creation of **Tempelhof Central Airport**, which was put into operation in 1923 and expanded up to the beginning of the second world war. This is still regarded as the largest inner city airport in the world – though its closure is nigh. The giant complex, created between 1936 and 1941 in line with the redesign of the Reich

capital by Albert Speer according to plans of Ernst Sagebiel, is with its central line oriented not, for example, to the Air Bridge Monument, but to the **Kreuzberg Monument**.

This national monument for the wars of liberation was set up between 1817 and 1821 according to plans by Karl Friedrich Schinkel and decorated by numerous, excellent sculptures of the members of the royal house and the generals. No less impressive is the view of the monument in the street canyon of Grossbeerenstrasse, in which there is a still imposing residential complex for the upper middle class dating from the early 20th c. between Yorck and Hagelberger Strasse with **Riemers Hofgarten**.

The park on the Kreuzberg is where the Kreuzberg festival takes place every autumn, which is when it's as lively as on Kreuzberg in the Berlin plain. That is to say: very lively.

Tempelhof Airport in the middle of the city is unique with its location and size (left). The Kreuzberg (above), which gave the surrounding district its name, reaches high up into the sky of Berlin.

103

East-West-scene

Eating & drinking

Abendmahl
Muskauer Strasse 9, international cuisine, daily 18–1, Tel: 612 51 70

Austria
Bergmannstrasse 30, Austrian cuisine, daily 18–1, June–Aug. from 19, cuisine until 24, Tel: 694 44 40

Chandra Kumari
Gneisenaustrasse 4, Indian cuisine, bio products from Sri Lanka, daily 12–1, food served until 0.30
Tel: 694 12 03

Chez Maurice
Bötzowstrasse 39, French cuisine, daily 18.30–24, Tel: 425 05 06

Chop-Bar
Pappelallee 29, African cuisine, Tues.–Sun. from 18, Tel: 44 03 62 76

Gugelhof
Knaackstrasse 37, Alsatian cuisine, daily 10–1, cuisine to 23.30,
Tel: 442 92 29

La Tana die Briganti
Oranienstrasse 169, Tuscan cuisine, large selection of wines
Mon.–Fr. from 11, Sat. from 18
Tel: 614 85 01

Mahanakhon
Herrfurthstrasse 31, Thai cuisine, daily 12–24, Set lunch 12–15
Tel: 622 25 93

Max und Moritz
Oranienstrasse 162, Berlin pub, daily 16–1, Tel: 614 10 45

Ostwind
Husemannstrasse 13, Far Eastern cuisine, Mon.–Fr. 18–1, Sat. and Sun. 11– 24, Tel: 441 59 51

Restaurant Svevo
Lausitzer Strasse 25, Tues.–Sun. From 18, August closed,
Tel: 61 07 32 16

Rice Queen
Danziger Strasse 13, Far Eastern cuisine, daily 17–24, Tel: 44 04 58 00

Shel Sushi Cocktailbar
Boxhagener Strasse 108, Mon–Sat. from 12, Sun. from 14,
Tel: 29 49 20 72

Treviso
Schönhauser Allee 12, Italian cuisine

in former Czech Embassy, daily 12–24 Tel: 44 01 73 33

Ypsilon – sushi & more
Metzer Strasse 30, please reserve at weekends, Tues.–Sat. 18–24,
Tel: 44 04 17 87

Shopping

Ackerhalle
Invalidenstrasse 159, Mon.–Fr. 8–20, Sat. –16

Benjowski Teehandelshaus (tea)
Danziger Strasse 3, Mon–Fr. 10–19, Sat. 10–14, Tel: 44 03 75 71

Boxhagener Platz
Fresh produce from the countryside, Thurs. 12–18, Sat. 8–13

Broken English
Körtestrasse 10, everything for an English breakfast, Mon –Fr. 11–18.30, Sat. 10–16, Tel: 691 12 27

Hallentrödelmarkt Treptow
(flea market)
Eichenstrasse 4, Sat. and Sun. 10–16

Kadó – Authentic flavours
Graefestrasse 75, licorice shop, Tues.–Fr. 9.30–18.30, Sat. 9–14,
Tel: 69 04 16 38

Karl-Marx-Platz, Turkish market
Sat. 8–13, Tel: 030-7815844

Kino am Kosmos
Karl-Marx-Allee 131a, international market, Mon., Wed. and Fr. 10–17

Knofi
Bergmannstrasse 98, vegetarian and vegand, Mon.–Fr. 8–20, Sat. 8–17,
Tel: 694 58 07

Kollwitzplatz, eco market with clothes, jewellery, food etc.
Thurs. 12–19, Sat. 9–16,
Tel: 030-44339136

Milchwirtschaft
Hufelandstrasse 17, cheeses, Mon.–Fr. 11–19, Sat. 9–14, Tel: 428 88 64, www.milchwirtschaft.de

Suff
Oranienstrasse 200, eco wine shop and delivery service for alcoholic beverages, Mon.–Fr. 13 – 19.30, Sat. 10 – 15, Tel: 61 45 21 48,
www.suffberlin.de

Turkish market on Maybachufer, little Istanbul, Tues. and Fr. 12–18.30

Wechselstube
Boxhagener Strasse 75, Portuguese pottery, action galleries, Mon.–Fr. 14–20, Sat. 12–16, Tel: 29 00 32 91

Sights

Gethsemanekirche
Stargarder Strasse 77, daily 9–17.30, Tel: 445 77 45

Jewish Cemetery
Schönhauser Allee 23-25

Kreuzberg Museum
Adalbertstrasse 95A, Wed.–Sun. 12–18, public holidays closed Tel: 50 58 52 33

Neue Gesellschaft für Bildende Kunst, Oranienstrasse 25, Mon.–Sun. 12–18.30, Tel: 615 30 31

Prenzlauer Berg Museum
Prenzlauer Allee 227-228, Tues. and Wed. 11–17, Thurs. 13–19 Sun. 14–18, Tel: 42 40 10 97

Sammlung Industrielle Gestaltung
Kulturbrauerei Knaackstrasse 97, Wed.–Sun. 13–20, Tel: 443 93 82

Gay Museum
Mehringsdamm 61, Wed.–Mon. 14–18, Sat. 14–19, Tel: 693 11 72

Rykestrasse Synagogue
Rykestrasse 53, after registration Tel: 442 59 31

Vitra Design Museum
Kopenhagener Strasse 58, Tues.–Sun. 11–20, Tel: 473 77 70

Zeiss Grossplanetarium
Prenzlauer Allee 80/Thälmannpark, Mon.–Fr. 10–12, Wed./Sat. 13.30 –21, Thurs./Fr. 18-22, Sun. 13.30–18, Tel: 42 18 45 12

Zionskirche
Zionskirchplatz, Sun. 12–16, Wed. 12–19, Thurs. 17–19, Tel: 449 21 91

Leisure

BKA-Theater
Mehringdamm 34, Tel: 251 01 12

Blub Freizeitparadies GmbH
Buschkrugallee 54, daily 10–23, Tel: 606 60 60, www.blub.berlin.de

Enoteca Bacco
Marheinekeplatz 15, wines and tapas, Vineria Mon. Fr. 9–19, Sat. 9–14, Enoteca 11–22 Sat. 11–17

Görlitzer Park at Görlitzer station

Hebbel-Theater, Stresemannstrasse 29, from 20, Tel: 25 90 04 27 www.hebbel-theater.de

Max-Schmeling-Halle
Am Falkplatz, sports events, Tel: 44 30 44 30, www.velomax.de

Volkspark Friedrichshain
Landsberger Allee

After 8

Frida Kahlo
Lychener Strasse 37, Central American cuisine, daily 10–2 Tel: 445 70 16

Drei
Lychener Strasse 30, bar with Californian/pan Asian cuisine, Mon.–Sat. 18–2, Sun. from 10, Tel: 44 73 84 71

Soda
Schönhauser Allee 36, restaurant, saloon, club, daily 10 -24 Tel: 44 05 87 08

Pfefferwerk
Schönhauser Allee 176, disco, concerts, Tel: 281 83 23

Die Busche
Mühlenstrasse 11, club Tel: 296 08 00

Fluido, Bar di Notte
Christburger Strasse 6, daily from 20, Tel: 44 04 39 02

Würgeengel
Dresdener Strasse 122, bar, daily from 19, Tel: 615 55 60

bat Studiotheater
Ernst Busch university for acting, Belforter Strasse 15, Tel: 442 76 13

Kulturbrauerei
Knaackstrasse 97, theatre, disco, concerts, Tel: 441 92 70

Bar Centrale
Yorckstrasse 82, Italian cuisine, Mon.–Thurs. 12–1, Fr. and Sat. 12–2, Sun. 12–1, Tel: 786 29 89

Prater
Kastanienallee 7-9, beer garden, theatre, popular fun, Tel: 448 56 88

Maria am Ostbahnhof
Strasse der Pariser Kommune 8-10, scene club, Tel: 283 12 52

Ufa-Fabrik, International Cultural Centre
Viktoriastrasse 10-18, Tel: 75 50 30

ROUTE 7

Berlin

The external areas of Berlin are not suburbs. They are the size of large towns and have more big city life than one might imagine.

Hamburg

ROUTE

Spandau

Havel

Wannsee

AROUND THE CENTRE

From the Funkturm to Strandbad Wannsee and from Pankow to Müggelsee

1 FUNKTURM FAIR GROUNDS
U Theodor-Heuss-Platz
BUS Messedamm/ICC

2 WANNSEE
S Wannsee

3 OLYMPIC STADIUM
U **S** Olympia Stadion

4 FRIEDRICHSFELDE PALACE
U Tierpark

5 KÖPENICK PALACE
S Köpenick

12 MÜGGELSEE
S **BUS** Köpenick

PUBLIC TRANSPORT
Flughafen Tegel:
Bus TXL, X 9, 109, 128
Altstadt Spandau: **U 2**
Olympia Stadion: **U 2, S 5, S 75**
Theodor-Heuss-Platz: **U 2**

BERLIN

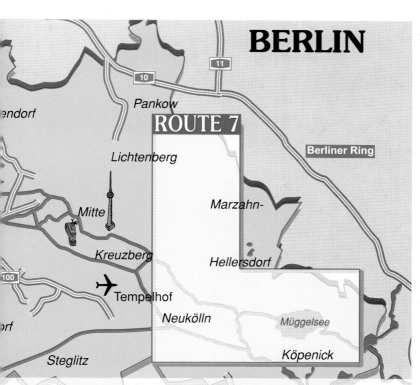

ROUTE 7

Pankow
Lichtenberg
Mitte
Kreuzberg
Marzahn-
Hellersdorf
Tempelhof
Neukölln
Müggelsee
Steglitz
Köpenick

Berliner Ring

Schönefeld

ssedamm: **Bus X 34, X 49, 139,**
9, X 21
unewaldturm: **Bus 218**
nnsee: **S 1**
xanderplatz: **U 2, U 5, U 8, S 3,**
, S 7, S 9, S 75, Tram 2, 3, 4, 5, 6,

Bus 2, 100, 142, 143, 148
Tierpark: **U 5**
Treptower Park: **S 4, S 6, S 8**
Köpenick: **S 3**
Köpenick: **Bus 69**

Albert Einstein no less held the speech at the opening of the **Funkturm** (Radio Tower) in 1926. Since then, the steel design, like a miniature version of the Eiffel Tower in Paris, has been a symbol of Berlin. Today the tower on the **Exhibition and Fair Grounds** is used only for police radio. On the other hand, the former Reichssportfeld with the **Olympic Stadium** in the centre and numerous competition and training facilities around about the over 130 ha Olympic site is still fully used in the original sense. A very fine view on city and environs is offered by the **Glockenturm**, 77 metre high, located on the edge of the giant Maifeld. From here, you also look on to the **Waldbühne**, built in the style of a amphitheatre and accommodating 20,000 visitors on 88 rows of seats.

From the Glockenturm, you can also see **Spandau**, which is older than Berlin and, in addition to possessing very extensive industrial areas, has a very quaint old town centre and, above all, the most Italian of all buildings in Berlin, the **Zitadelle**. This bull-like

The Funkturm (left), built in 1924–26, is 150 metres high right up to the tip of the aerial. It is located in the centre of the fair grounds and very near the Avus, built in 1921. The Olympic Stadium (below) was created for the Olympic Games in summer 1936.

fortress boasting four bastions sited at the mouth of the Spree into the Havel was built at the end of the 16th c. modelled on Italian designs and served as a fortress only in 1813 in the wars of liberation. Otherwise it functioned as munitions depot, treasure vault and prison. Today it's a unique monument, over which you can hear the roar of the aircraft taking off and landing at Tegel Airport when there's a west wind and from where you can admire, even if only briefly, the beauty of the landscape around **Tegeler See**, on the northern end of which is **Humboldt Palace**.

The Zitadelle (above) is Spandau's symbol. Tegel Airport (centre) is the largest of the three airports in the city. Tegel Palace (below), also called Humboldt Palace, was designed by the architect Karl Friedrich Schinkel.

The Plötzensee Memorial recalls those who were executed here by guillotine or hanging during the Third Reich.

The **Plötzensee Memorial** on the site of a former Nazi state prison south-west of Tegel Airport. A total of 2,500 people were executed here up to April 25th 1945 as supposed enemies of the state.

The sights are less brutal on the northern and eastern outskirts of the city.

In the north, there are **Niederschönhausen Palace** and Niederschönhausen Park, in which the wife of Friedrich the Great lived for 47 years as outcast, the large **Jewish cemetery** in Weissensee and the **Mies van der Rohe House** on Obersee in Hohenschönhausen.

Niederschönhausen Palace (early 18th c.) in the district Pankow

A garden of a quite distinctive character has been created in Marzahn (above). Lovers of equestrian sport are attracted to Hoppegarten (below centre), animal lovers to the Tierpark with Friedrichsfelde Palace (below).

In the east there are the giant new residential areas in **Hellersdorf** and **Marzahn** and in the middle of this landscape of concrete panels the Marzahn recreation park with a particularly attractive **China Garden** – and even further outside, already outside the city border, the racecourse **Hoppegarten**, in the city area the Karlshorst trotting course and half way between the racing courses the spacious **Tierpark Berlin** (opened in 1955), into which the over 300-year-old Friedrichsfelde Palace is integrated.

Berlin

Potsdam

BERLIN

from the water

STEAMER TRIPS

Spandau

Wannsee

POTSDAM

Berlin is located where it now is because it was where the Spree and the marshes could be crossed. Today you can traverse the city and even go around it by water. The federal waterways in the Berlin city area have an overall length of 165.7 km.

The shortest of these, the Dahme waterway near Schmöckwitz, is just 1,000 metres long; the longest, the Spree-Oder waterway, 46.8 km. All these are used by barges as well as passenger ships of Stern und Kreis Schiffahrt, which has numerous landing stages throughout the city area and can thus take passengers leisurely through Berlin, under bridges and into locks so that they can admire the city or just enjoy the head wind and sitting in the sun.

LANDING PLACES

1) Wannsee
2) Kladow
3) Spandau
4) Alt-Tegel
5) Schlossbrücke
6) Tegeler Weg
7) Treptower Park
8) Müggelsee/
   Köpenick
9) Potsdam

PUBLIC TRANSPORT

Wannsee: **S 1, S 7**
Kladow: **Bus Alt Kladow X 34**
Spandau: **U 7 Altstadt Spandau**
Alt-Tegel: **U 6 Alt-Tegel**
Schlossbrücke:
Bus **"Schlossbrücke" X 21, 109**
Tegeler Weg:
Bus **"Osnabrücker Strasse" X 21,**
109

Treptower Park:
S 4, S 6, S 8, S 9, S 85,
Bus "Treptower Park" 104, 166,
167, 194, 265
Müggelsee/Köpenick:
S 3 "Köpenick", Bus "Müggel-
schlösschenweg" X 69
Potsdam: **S 7 "Potsdam HBF"**

The Müggelsee with its numerous tributary waters, the nature reserve in the east of Berlin

Berlin isn't the concrete jungle suggested by the development of its inner city areas. Of its close on 890 km², as much as a third is forest or green area, 6.8 percent agriculturally usable land and 6.4 percent water – which is a great deal for a city with about 3.4 million inhabitants.

Although Berlin isn't a city in green surroundings, but a city on the water: in the west the large Havel lakes and in the east the lakes fed by the Spree and its tributaries.

The district of **Köpenick** in the south-east of Berlin is the most densely forested and has the most lakes and is also the most thinly populated district of the city. Of its area of close on 130 km², nearly 55 percent is forest and parks and amost 16 percent water areas.

The district is thinly populated the

Steamer landing stage at Grosser Müggelsee

entire year, but full almost every weekend.

The forests and lakes are a unique nature reserve that is so spacious there is no risk of not being able to see the forest what with all the trippers and hikers, picknickers and joggers.

Köpenick is also still a town that achieved a certain national fame as a result of the impostor "Hauptmann von Köpenick", who was actually a shoemaker by the name of Voigt.

It's worth seeing the late 17th c. **palace**, in which there is now a branch of the **Arts and Crafts Museum**, along with the palace church and palace park from the same period and, of course, the town hall built at the beginning of the 20th c. – in 1906 this was the scene of the roguish trick of Voigt, who ventured to play fast and loose with the Prussian subservient mentality.

The Müggelturm (below l.) tops the Kleiner Müggelberg, 92 metres high. Köpenick Palace (below) graces the district of the same name.

Attractions in the south-west: the Botanical Gardens (above) and the numerous museums in Dahlem, including the Ethnological Museum (below)

What the Müggel lakes are in the east of Berlin, the Havel lakes are in the west: a wonderful nature reserve. On the way from one summer pleasure to another – or, in winter, from one ice rink to the other – you pass in the south of Berlin the **Botanical Gardens**, the **Dahlem museums** and the spacious site of the **Free University**. The Botanical Gardens in Steglitz were created between 1897 and

The Havel lakes on the edge of the Grunewald, the largest nature reserve in the west of Berlin

Strandbad Wannsee, still the largest open-air swimming pool in Europe

1910 as replacement for the Botanical Gardens in the city centre coming more and more under the new buildings. There was space here outside, at that time still outside the city area. Today the garden with its 18,000 species of plant on 48 ha is one of the largest in the world. It features a 25 metre high tropical house, an outstanding work of glass-steel architecture of the late 19th c., in its centre. In addition to the Museum Island, the Cultural Forum and the collections in and at Charlottenburg Palace, the Dahlem museums are an important museum centre in Berlin. The Ethnological Museum is located here, and witnesses of the cultures India, East Asia, Africa and North America are exhibited here in the museum buildings, which were created only after the second world war.

The Free University, founded in December 1948 in Titania Palace in Steglitz as an alternative to the politicizing of Humboldt University in the centre, has constantly grown in the immediate vicinity of the museums.

Dahlem isn't very far from **Grosser Wannsee**, an approx. 240 ha large bulge in the Havel.

On the western edge of this bay is **Strandbad Wannsee**, created in 1929–30 in the style of the "New Objectivity" movement with a 1,275 metre long and up to 80 metre wide sandy beach. If everyone moves up closer together a little, there's enough space for over 50,000 swimmers or also only sun worshippers. There were as many as 53,000 on 1.6.1947, which is still the record for one day.

From here, we reach upriver first Spandau and then Tegel, downriver the town of palaces and gardens, Potsdam, which with the Pfaueninsel announces itself early on. Although this island is in Berlin, it belongs to Potsdam.

Addresses from the Funkturm to Strandbad Wannsee

Eating & drinking

Eisvogel
Motzener Strasse 30, ice café,
Mon.–Sat. 6–22, in summer also Sun.
8–16, Tel: 723 00 70

Gasthaus Feuerbach
Schöneberger Strasse 14,
Mon.–Thurs. 9–1, Fr. and Sat. 9–3,
Sun. 10–1, Tel: 85 07 54 84

Kang Feng
Manfred-von-Richthofen-Strasse 6
Chinese cuisine, daily 11.30–24,
Tel: 77 00 85 18

Konditorei Fester (confectioner's)
Spandau market, Mon.–Fr. 8–20, Sat.
8–18, Sun. 13–19 Tel: 333 58 72

Remise
Königstrasse 36, Tel: 805 40 00

Shopping

Spandau old town
Carl-Schurz-Strasse, market, Wed.
8–18, Sat. 8–16, Tel: 33 03 22 78

Autos & Weine (cars and wine)
Willmanndamm 18, Mon.–Fr. 10–19,
Sat. 10–15, Tel: 7881200
www. cars -weine.de

Bunzlauer Landhauskeramik
(pottery)
Hohenzollerndamm 197, Mon.–Fr.
11–18, Wed. 10–18, Sat. 9–13,
Tel: 873 29 57

Der verrückte Laden
(The Mad Shop)
Bürgerheimstrasse 19, gifts,
Mon.–Fr. 10–18.30, Sat. 10–13, Tel:
57 79 52 38

IKEA
Ruhlebener Strasse 23, Mon.–Fr.
9.30–20, Sat. 8.30–16
Tel: 0180-5353435

Köpenicker Bauernmarkt
Schüsslerplatz, Tues. and Thurs.
9–17.30, Tel: 65 82 27 30

Kranoldplatz
Wochenmarkt, Wed. and Sat. 8–13

Lisa's leckere Marmeladen (jams)
Clayallee 68, Mon.–Fr. 9–19
Sat. 9–16, Sun. 10–18 Tel: 831 41 92
www.lisa-marmeladen.de

Nature department store
Schlossstrasse 101, biological and
ecological products, Mon.–Fr. 10–20,
Sat. 10–16, Tel: 797 37 16

Nuevo Mundo
Zimmermannstrasse 31, Chilean wi-
nes, Mon.–Fr. 15–20, Sat. 11–15,
Tel: 0179-5294763

Peak
Wilhelminenhofstrasse 88, Ober-
schöneweide, trekking accessories
Mon.–Fr. 10–20, Sat. 10–16,
Tel: 53 78 05 17

Stoff
Westfälische Strasse 27, children's
toys, ecological and natural,
Mon.–Fr. 10–13 and 15–18, Sat.
10–13, Tel: 89 09 44 22

Sights

Allied Museum
Clayallee, Thurs.–Tues. 10-18
Tel: 81 81 990

Anna Seghers Memorial
Anna-Seghers-Strasse 81,
Tues./Wed. 10–16, Thurs. 10–18
Tel: 677 47 25

Botanical Gardens
Königin-Luise-Strasse 6, Nov.–Jan.
9–16, Feb. 9–17, March and Oct.
9–18, April and Aug. 9–20, May–July
9–21 Tel: 83 85 01 00

Botanical Museum
Königin-Luise-Strasse 6-8, daily
10–18, Tel: 83 85 01 00
www.bgbm.fu-berlin.de

Brücke Museum
Bussardsteig 9, Wed.–Mon. 11–17,
Tel: 831 20 29

Chinese Garden
Eisenacher Strasse 99, daily 9–17,
Tel: 54 69 80, www.gruen-berlin.de

Ethnological Museum
Lansstrasse 8, Tues.–Fr. 10–18,
Sat./Sun. 11–18, Tel: 830 14 38

Hohenschönhausen Memorial
Genslerstrasse 66, former GDR
remand prison (NKWD and MfS),
only with guide, Mon.–Sun. 11 and
13 and by agreement
Tel: 98 60 82 30, www.gedenkstaet-
te-hohenschoenhausen.de

Plötzensee Memorial
Hüttigpfad, March–Oct. daily 9–17,
Tel: 344 32 26

Georg Kolbe Museum
Sensburger-Allee 25, Tues.–Sun.
10–17, Tel: 304 21 44

Gründerzeitmuseum (1870s)
Hultschiner Damm 333, Charlotte
von Mahlsdorf, Wed. and Sun.
10–18, Tel: 56 59 48 72

Haus am Waldsee
Argentinische Allee 30, various exhi-
bitions, Tues.–Sun. 12–20
Tel: 63 21 52 34

House of the Wannsee conference
Am Grossen Wannsee 56-58, daily
10–18, Tel: 805 00 10,
www.ghwk.de

Weissensee Jewish Cemetery
Herbert-Baum-Strasse 45
Air Force Museum of the Federal
Armed Forces
Flugplatz Gatow, Kladower Damm,
Tues.–Sun. 9–17, Tel: 36 87 26 01
Mies van der Rohe House
Oberseestrasse 60, Tues.–Thurs.
13–18 Sat./Sun. 14–18,
Tel: 97 00 06 18
Museum Berlin Karlshorst
Zwieseler Strasse, changing
exhibitions, Tues.–Sun. 10–18
Tel: 50 15 08 10
Museum of European Cultures
Im Winkel, Tues.–Fr. 10–18,
Sat./Sun. 11–18, Tel: 83 90 12 87
Museum for Indian Art
Lansstrasse 8, Tues.–Fr. 10–18, Sat.
and Sun. 11–18, Tel: 830 13 61
Museum for East Asian Art
Lansstrasse 8, Tues.–Fr. 10–18,
Sat./Sun. 11–18, Tel: 830 13 82
Naturschutzzentrum Schleipfuhl
Hermsdorfer Strasse 11a, low-energy
house, Tues. 8–16, Wed. and Thurs.
8–18 Tel: 998 91 84 www.natur-
schutz-bahnhof-malchow.de
Britz Palace
Altw-Britz 73, Tues.–Thurs. 14–18,
Fr. 14–20, Tel: 60 97 92 30
Tegel Palace
Adelheidallee 19-21, visit only with
guide, Mon. 10, 11, 15 and 16,
Tel: 434 31 56
Pfaueninsel Palace and Landscape
Garden
Garden daily 10–16, palace
April–Oct. Tues.–Sun. 10–13 and
13.30–17, Tel: 80 58 66 30
Sportforum Hohenschönhausen
Konrad-Wolf-Strasse 45, sport
events, ice rink, venue of the
Berliner Eisbären, Tel: 97 17 00
Friedrichsfelde Central Cemetery
Gudrunstrasse, memorial of the
socialist von Mies van der Rohe,
open at all hours, Tel: 559 75 33
Zitadelle Spandau
Am Juliusturm, Tues.–Fr. 9–17,
Sat./Sun. 10–17, Tel: 354 94 42 00
Sugar Museum
Amrumer Strasse 32, Mon.–Thurs.
9–16.30, Sun. 11–18, Tel: 31 42 75 74
Leisure
ASPRIA Berlin
Karlsruher Strasse 20, fitness and
wellness, Mon.–Fr. 6–23, Sat.,
Sun. and public holidays 9-22
Tel: 890 68 88 10, www.aspria.de

Berlin Arena
Paul-Heyse-Strasse 26, various sport
events,
Tel: 61 10 13 13 or 44 30 44 30
carrousel Theater an der Parkaue
children's theatre, An der Parkaue
29, Tel: 55 77 52 52,
www.carousel.de
Funkturm on the Fair Grounds
Messedamm 22, lookout platform,
Mon. 11–21, Tues. –Sun. 10–22,
restaurant Tues.–Sun. 11.30–22,
Tel: 30 38 29 96
Weissensee Academy of Art
Bühringstrasse 20, Tel: 47 70 53 42
www.kh-berlin.de
Museum of Prohibited Art in old
watchtower
Im Schlesischen Busch, Sat. and
Sun. 12–18
Schöneberg town hall
John-F.-Kennedy-Platz, daily 10–18,
tower daily 10–16, Tel: 756 00
Köpenick Palace
Müggelheimer Strasse 1
Tel: 20 90 55 66
Pfaueninsel Palace and Landscape
Garden
Jan. and Feb. 10–16, March 9–17,
April 8–18, May–Aug. 8–20 Sept.
8–18, Oct. 9–17, Nov. and Dec. 10
–16 Tel: 0331-9694202,
www.spsg.de
Strandbad Wannsee
Wannseebadweg 25, Mon.–Fr.
10–19, Sat. and Sun. 8–20,
Tel: 01803-102020,
www.bbb.berlin.de
Tierpark Friedrichsfelde
Am Tierpark 125, summer daily
9–19, winter daily 9–17, Tel: 51 53 10
Karlshorst Trotting Course
Treskowallee 129, Tel: 50 01 71 21
www.berlintrab.de
Mariendorf Trotting Course
Mariendorfer Damm 222, racing the
whole year, Tel: 740 12 12
After 8
Kiste
Heidenauer Strasse 10, film evenings,
dance festivals, readings, concerts,
admission, Tel: 998 74 81
Parkbühne Wuhlheide
An der Wuhlheide, open-air theatre
Tel: 53 07 91 00
Parkhaus
Puschkinallee 5, jazz cellar
Tel: 533 79 52
Waldbühne, Glockenturmstrasse 1
Tel: 23 08 82 30, www.deag.de

ROUTE 8

Berlin

Potsdam

POTSDAM

Town of palaces and gardens

HIGHLIGHTS

BERLIN POTSDAM
BUS S

1 CECILIENHOF
BUS Cecilienhof

2 SANSSOUCI
BUS Sanssouci – Historische Mühle

3 BRANDENBURGER TOR
BUS Tram Luisenplatz

4 NIKOLAIKIRCHE/STADTHAUS
BUS Tram Am Kanal,
Platz der Einheit

5 NEUES PALAIS
BUS Wildpark

6 NAUENER TOR
BUS Tram Nauener Tor

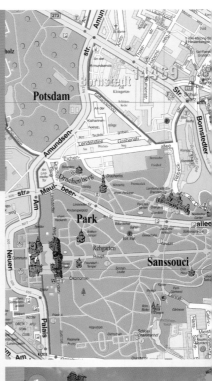

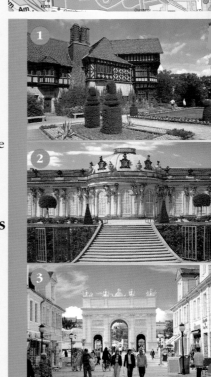

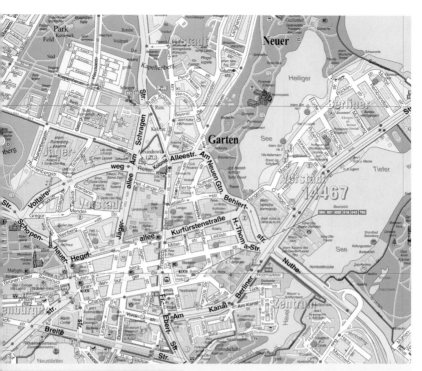

Potsdam stands for more than just a town: Potsdam begins as a cultural landscape where it actually is no longer town. That has been the case for three centuries.

PUBLIC TRANSPORT

Berlin Potsdam:
S 7 (Westkreuz, Potsdam Hbf)
Cecilienhof: **Bus 692**
Sanssouci – Historische Mühle:
Bus 695
Luisenplatz: **Tram 04, 06, Bus 580, 631, 695**
Am Kanal/Platz der Einheit:
Bus N 16, Tram 03
Wildpark: **Bus 606, 695**
Nauener Tor: **Bus 692, Tram 02, 06**

It isn't known since when the **Pfaueninsel** has swum in the Havel. But we do know that from about 1685 it became a place of banishment and then a safe haven and a refuge. First the Great Elector banished the alchemist, glassmaker and wizard Johann Kunkel with the order to invent something beautiful. But that didn't work out. Friedrich Wilhelm II purchased the island a hundred years later, in 1793. He had already visited it previously, as king, as successor to the throne and above all as lover

of the young Wilhelmine Enke, daughter of a court musician, whom he made pregnant and whose children he resolutely supported contrary to the usual practice at the court. He had a tiny palace built for his mistress on the island which is ruin and façade at the same time. Inside and outside, it has remained as it was. From the turret, Wilhelmine could have waved to the king, who resided in the **Marble Palace** and perhaps she did.

The Marble Palace in the **New Garden** is a defiant reaction. Scarcely had Friedrich II been buried than his successor Friedrich Wilhelm II used up the marble stored in the building depot for this little palace very close to the edge of the **Heiliger See** and on the edge of the New Garden, in which many exciting and enigmatic structures were created within ten years: the **palace kitchen** in the form of a half sunk temple ruin poking up out of the lake, an **obelisk** with medallions of the four seasons, a **pyramid**,

The Pfaueninsel with its ornate palace (above) as well as Glienecke Palace (below) is now in Berlin, but belongs to the Potsdam cultural heritage.

which was used as an ice cellar and adorned with far more hieroglyphics than it is today, and finally, at the southern end of Heiliger See, a neo-Gothic library by Langhans, the original counterpart of a Moorish temple demolished in 1869 at the opposite end of the lake.

The Marble Palace on Heiliger See (above and right) and in the New Garden (below), which also includes the Gothic Library (below right).

Cecilienhof Palace, built during the first world war, was the venue of the Potsdam conference at the end of the second world war. It is the last Hohenzollern palace building.

Cecilienhof Palace, today a hotel and museum, the last palace building of Prussian history is in the New Garden below the Pfingstberg with the **Belvedere** and

Pomonatempel, the first building of Karl Friedrich Schinkel. Cecilienhof, which was not completed until 1917 for Crown Prince Wilhelm, is a half-timbered complex built around several courtyards in the style of an English country estate with an elegant interior behind the rustic façade. The **Potsdam Treaty** was sealed in the building in 1945 by the four Allied victorious powers, which convened here in Potsdam and not in Berlin because Cecilienhof was a venue with a roof that was easy to secure.

The town is west and south of the New Garden, even if on the edges, such as in **Bornstedt** in former crown estate, on the **Kapellenberg** with the Russian orthodox church and in the **Alexandrowka colony** in front of Nauener Tor, it has a rather rural feeling.

But the town begins behind the massive **Nauener Tor** (1755) with the impressive Dutch Quarter, created for Dutch craftsmen between 1734 and 1742. Only they knew how to build on marshy ground. Today the houses are an attractive feature of Potsdam.

The town of Potsdam consists not only of palaces and gardens: its sights also include the church in Bornstedt (right, above), the Kapellenberg with the orthodox church of St. Alexander Newski (right, centre), Nauener Tor (below, left) and the Dutch Quarter (below, right).

Brandenburger Strasse with Brandenburger Tor (above) is Potsdam's shopping street. The French Church (below, centre) is at Bassinplatz. The old market with the old town hall (below) was the original centre of the town.

Potsdam never had a chance to become a nice little town in beautiful surroundings, also sometimes blessed with beautiful weather. It was created by the military, bore the stamp by the military and was also partially destroyed by the military.

In the late evening of July 14th 1945 – exactly 200 years after the laying of the foundation stone for Sanssouci Palace – 490 Royal Air Force bombers raided the town: thousands were killed, entire streets of houses burnt down, 856 houses were completely and 248 partially destroyed and 3,301 buildings damaged. The historic centre of Potsdam around the palace and old market were bombed beyond recognition that night. The British official army communiqué reported: "Potsdam no longer exists."

The centre of the old town, which no longer exists, still has the **Nikolaikirche**, **old town hall**, **Marstall**, a colonnade, once linking the palace with the Marstall, the obelisk and a freshly built palace portal, as if to make us wish for more palace on this square, on which the city palace used to stand before being pulled down in 1959. The present centre of the city is formed by Friedrich-Ebert-Strasse plus the side streets and **Brandenburger Strasse**, expanded into a pedestrian zone ending with **Brandenburger Tor**, not far from Sanssouci Park.

On the far side of the gate there is already the green trellis of the Marlygarten, which Friedrich Wilhelm I had created as kitchen garden, and the mid-19th c. **Friedenskirche** by Persius. From here, it's only a few steps to the vineyard terrace with Sanssouci Palace and the large fountain, fed

The pumping station for Sanssouci (above) in the bend of the Havel around the new town is a reference to Sanssouci Palace (see following double page). The Marly Garden (centre) and Friedenskirche (below) are on the edge of Sanssouci Park.

by the Moorish-looking pumping station in the bend of the Havel around the new town.

The sunny side of Sanssouci Palace: here Friedrich II and his dogs have their final resting place. In the palace, baroque exuberance is confined not just to the marble hall (centre) and the Voltaire Room (below).

Sanssouci Palace is the most beautiful, most exciting and also most individual building designed by Georg Wenzeslaus Konobels-dorff. It deights us not only with the contrast, also realized else-where, between a cool classicist outer building and the most extra-vagant rococo inner rooms, giving the flat and intimate a building a magnificent as well as cheerful note. The palace, in fact, has two faces: from the court side with its classicist **colonnade** of 88 Corinthian columns, one can hard-ly suspect the design of the garden side. The style is very severe towards the **Ruinenberg** (Hill of Ruins), but downright exuberant to the south, to the **vineyard ter-race**, where no columns bear the attika crowned with vases; highly vivaciously crafted bacchants and bacchantes prop up the timber-work with drunken casualness. The opulence of the garden side of the palace is continued in the interior in the rooms on both sides of the central marble hall. The

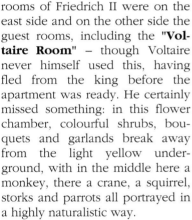

rooms of Friedrich II were on the east side and on the other side the guest rooms, including the **"Voltaire Room"** – though Voltaire never himself used this, having fled from the king before the apartment was ready. He certainly missed something: in this flower chamber, colourful shrubs, bouquets and garlands break away from the light yellow underground, with in the middle here a monkey, there a crane, a squirrel, storks and parrots all portrayed in a highly naturalistic way.

Encores to this truly unique building are the **New Chambers** (1747) to the west, which were first orangery and then guest-house, and on the other side the **Painting Gallery** (1755), one of the early galleries, which from the outside suggests nothing of its giant exhibition hall for paintings.

The park below Sanssouci Palace is full of sights, which sometimes, if you know about its history, are also curiosities. Take the **Large Fountain.** Friedrich II 1748 had

Sanssouci Palace, flanked by the painting gallery (top right and centre) and New Chambers with windmill

Chinese House in Sanssouci Park – sans any trace of a typical Prussian spirit

the idea of creating a large water reservoir above the palace – the **Ruinenberg** with its artificial ruin architecture is actually nothing other than this – but it didn't prove to be possible to pump water from the Havel into the reservoir, which was 45 metres higher, so he shelved the project in 1763. It wasn't until 1842 that water flowed through the **pumping station** on the Havel, disguised as a mosque in contemporary style, also into the royal garden.

On the other hand, the **Chinese House** (1754–56), is very exuberant. It has three cabinets connected by loggias grouped around a round central hall adorned with exquisite fantastic paintings on a cloverleaf ground-plan. Stone people – which make the observer an almost indiscreet spectator of their doings – sit in the loggias. The curved roof, which puffs itself here and there like the tented roofs of former chairoplanes, seems to be in motion. But a self-satisfied grinning mandarin with a sunshade squats on the roof, right on top of the lantern.

On the other hand, the **Roman Baths**, built by Schinkel and Per-

The cool outer austerity of the Roman Baths, built according to plans by Karl Friedrich Schinkel and Ludwig Persius, is misleading: inside (below) it's merry and ornate.

sius between 1829 and 1836, are of downright cool severity, modelled on an the Italian villa style of the time, which aimed at an orderly life of idling – bathing, meditating and playing billiards and indulging in tall stories at most on the side: for instance, the flounder as gargoyle in the so-called large gardenhouse and the flounder as decor on the china crockery. "Butt" (Flounder") was the nickname of the crown prince, later king Friedrich Wilhelm IV.

The **Meierei** (dairy) is located to the north and built in a style similar to the Roman Baths and the **Pheasantry** located to the west, the last building to be built in the park around Charlottenhof Palace. Between 1826 and 1828, Karl Friedrich Schinkel along with landscape planner and gardener Peter Joseph Lenné set a little work of art in the heath landscape, which was at that time weeded

over and in which there wasn't even a trickle, south of the Friede-

Charlottenhof Palace was created very much in the spirit of the romantic classical age: from the artificial lake outside to the blue tent room (below) in the interior.

Orangery, originally built as a guest-house

rich Rehgarten (Deer Park). This was Charlottenhof Palace with an artificial lake, which was passed on to Crown Prince Friedrich Wilhelm.

He called the palace including the neighbouring Roman Baths "Siam" and wanted it to be regarded as a "Land of the Free", as a vision of a better world, which can scarcely reconcile its strange beauty with

From the Belvedere on the Klausberg (right), you can look straight to Sanssouci Palace and the New Palace. The Dragon House (left), today a café, was originally a winegrower's house.

Prussian reality. It was Friedrich Wilhelm's intention, Lenné has recounted, "not actually to live in" the palace. He wanted it only as an art landscape full of naturalness. It was also designed for dreams and less for living inside: the rooms for courtly relationships downright tiny, but with choice furniture and handicrafts and in the middle, a cavern just as children like building in parental apartments, the **blue tent room**, actually intended for the ladies-in-waiting, but used as guest room.

The buildings that were then built during the regency of Friedrich Wilhelm lack such elegance and balance: the **New Orangery** north of Maulbeerallee, created between 1851 and 1860, is pretty massive with its 300 metre long front.

Sights worth seeing here on the slight rise are the **Dragon House**, located further to the west, and the **Belvedere** with a view of the **New Palace**. On the way there, you pass underneath the Dragon House a **miniature fortress** built for the sons of Kaiser Wilhelm II.

Between the **New Palace** at the end of Sanssouci Park and Charlottenhof Palace there are 800 metres, 60 years and worlds. Charlottenhof, small and fine – the New Palace plus the **Communs** behind, both built up to 1769, large and ostentatious, as if Friedrich II wanted to show the world power and glory. The building cost a pretty 2,860,177 talers – nine times the cost of Sanssouci, and four times the price tag of the town palace. For this sum, a 240 metre long palace with 300 rooms, 322 windows, 230 pilasters and

480 figures in front of and on the façade was created. The interior decoration extending right into the wonderful small **baroque theatre** is no less opulent. The only problem was the statics of the main festive hall, the marble hall extending over two floors: dancing in the court society was forbidden here right from the beginning because of the risk of the building collapsing.

Babelsberg Palace was the result of a great deal of pestering in the house of the Hohenzollerns. All of them already had their little palaces – Prince Carl at Glienicker bridge, Prince Friedrich Wilhelm in Charlottenhof – only Prince Wilhelm, who was to become later the first Emperor of the German Reich, made along with Princess Augusta plans that came to nothing time and time again because of paternal thrift.

In 1833, the pair finally obtained permission from Friedrich Wilhelm III to have a small cottage built by

The New Palace on the western end of Sanssouci Park, a splendid complex from the outside. Al its halls and rooms, including its theatre, are lavishly decorated.

Schinkel on Babelsberg. Babelsberg Palace was thus created in two sections in romantic/neo-Gothic style on a beautiful site above the Havel.

Although during the construction phases the princess didn't display much taste, she was certainly able to get her way. She had a turret and oriel in over-elaborate decorated style installed during the conversion of the **Damenhaus** (Little Palace), and on her suggestion the **Matrosenhaus** (Sailors' House) was given a front that is nothing other than the imitation of the gable on the Stendal town hall. The park was designed by two grand masters: First from Peter Joseph Lenné and then Hermann Fürst von Pückler.

The park itself is dominated by the massive **Flatow Tower**, 46 metre high, built with stones from the former princely domain in Flatow in West Prussia.

The early Gothic **court building** of the old Berlin town hall, with which the Berliners didn't want to have anything more to do when building the red town hall and which was brought to Potsdam at the command of Kaiser Wilhelm I, is also in the park.

But the most beautiful view of Potsdam is to be had from the **Victoriahöhe** in the south-west of the park. From here, at the base of a triumphal column crowned by a

bronze Victoria by Christian Daniel Rauch, you have Potsdam with all its beauties and high spirits at your feet.

Babelsberg Palace, summer seat of Prince and later Kaiser Wilhelm I, above the lake Glienicker See

There are buildings of very different kinds in Babelsberg Park: the Small Palace (below, far left), Matrosenhaus (below, left), court building (below) and massive Flatow Tower (right).

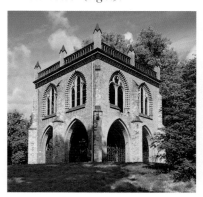

Potsdam (dialling code: 0331)

Eating & drinking

Arco in Nauener Tor
Italian cuisine, Friedrich-Ebert-Strasse, Tel: 270 16 90

Bagels & Coffee
Friedrich-Ebert-Strasse 92
Tel: 887 16 12

Barokoko
Mediterranean cuisine, Friedrich-Ebert-Strasse 30, Tel: 280 14 38

Bürgerstuben
German cuisine, Jägerstrasse 10
Tel: 280 11 09

Café Heider
Friedrich-Ebert-Strasse,
Tel: 270 55 96

Café in Film Museum
Breite Strasse, Tel: 270 20 41

Dolce Vita, Italian cuisine, Wilhelm Gallery, Tel: 201 16 00

El Puerto, Hafen an der Langen Brücke, Tel: 275 92 95

Froschkasten
Kiezstrasse 3-4, Tel: 29 13 15

Kartoffel Pub (Potato Pub)
Grossbeerenstrasse 107,
Tel: 71 01 59

La Maison du Chocolat
Benkertstrasse 20, Tel: 237 07 30

Lehmofen
Anatolian specialities, Hermann-Elflein-Strasse 10, Tel: 280 17 12

Socher`s
Alpine cuisine, Charlottenstrasse 13,
Tel: 58 92 77

Restaurant Persius Mühle
regional and international cuisine,
Zeppelinstrasse 136, Tel: 909 88 13

Restaurant Zur Historischen Mühle
Zur historischen Mühle 2
Tel: 28 14 93

Ristorante Fellini
Lindenstrasse 6, Tel: 299 79 52

Seerose
Breite Strasse 24, Tel: 97 41 17

Villa Kellermann
Mangerstrasse 34-36, Tel: 29 15 72

Waldcafé
Heinrich-Mann-Allee 69 Tel: 87 91 29

Shopping

Floh- und Bauernmarkt
Weberplatz, Sat. 8–14

Jürgen Trubel
grocer's, Lindenstrasse 10

Königsblau Keramik
Mittelstrasse 7

Krongut Bornstedt
regional products, Ribbeckstrasse 6/7

Wochenmarkt (weekly market)
Bassinplatz, Mon.–Fr. 7–17, Sat. 7–12

Sights

Belvedere on Pfingstberg
(New Garden), Tel: 270 19 72

Berliner S-Bahn (City Transit) Museum
Rudolf-Breitscheid-Strasse 203, tours by agreement, Tel: 030-78 70 55 11

Painting Gallery (Sanssouci)
May 15th–Oct. 15th Tues.–Sun.
10–12.30 and 13–17, Tel: 96 94 181

Biosphere in Buga-Park Potsdam
Georg-Hermann-Allee 99
Tel:55 07 40 Fax: 55 07 420
E-mail: info@biosphare.de
Internet: www.biosphaere.net

Botanical Gardens of Potsdam University
Maulbeerallee 2, outdoor area:
April–Oct. 7–17, greenhouses:
April–Sept. 9.30–17,
Oct.–March 9.30–16
Tel: 977 19 52, Fax: 977 19 51

Chinese House (Sanssouci)
May 15th–Oct. 15th Tues.–Sun.
10–12.30 and 13–17, Tel: 96 94 222

Ladies' Wing in Sanssouci Palace
May 15th–Oct. 15th Sat./Sun.
10–12.30 and 13–17, Tel: 96 94 184

Dampfmaschinenhaus (steam engines)
Breite Strasse, May 15th–Oct. 15th
Sat./Sun. 10–12.30 and 13–17,
Tel: 96 94 248

Flatow Tower (Babelsberg Park)
April 1st–Oct. 27th Sat./Sun. 10–17,
Tel: 96 94 249

Friedenskirche (Sanssouci)
May–Oct. daily 10–18, Tel: 97 40 09

Lindenstrasse Memorial
Former remand prison of the GDR
state security police, Tues., Thurs.
and every, 1st and 3rd Sat. in month
9–17 Tel: 289 61 31

House of Brandenburg-Prussian History
Kutschstall, Neuer Markt,
Tel: 201 393; reopening in autumn 2003

Hiller-Brandtsche Häuser
Breite Strasse 8-12, Tel: 289 66 00-03
temporarily closed

Historische Mühle (Sanssouci)
April–Oct. daily 10–18

Nov.–March Sat./Sun. 10–16
Tel: 96 94 284
Jagdschloss Stern
Jagdhausstrasse, tour only with
registered guide, Tel: 96 94 240
Jan Bourman House
Mittelstrasse 8, Mon., Tues., Thurs.,
Fr. 13–18, Sat./Sun. 11–18
Tel: 280 37 73, Fax: 280 58 72
Krongut Bornstedt
Ribbeckstrasse 6/7, E-mail:
info@krongut-bornstedt.de
Internet: www.krongut-bornstedt.de
Marble Palace (New Garden)
April–Oct. Tues.–Sun. 10–17
Nov.–March Sat./Sun. 10–16
Tel: 96 94 246
Natural History Museum
Breite Strasse 13, Tues.–Sun. 9–17
Tel: 289 66 00
New Chambers (Sanssouci)
April–May 14th Sat./Sun. 10–17, May
15th–Oct. 15th Tues. – Sun.
10–12.30 and 13–17, Tel: 96 94 206
New Palace (Sanssouci)
April–Oct. Sat.–Thurs. 9–17
Nov. – March Sat.–Thurs. 9–16
Tel: 96 94 255
Orangerieschloss (Sanssouci)
May 15th–Oct. 15th Tues.–Sun.
10–12.30 and 13–17, Tel: 96 94 222
Pomonatempel (New Garden)
Auf dem Pfingstberg, April–Oct.
Sat./Sun. 15–18, Tel: 270 19 72
Roman Baths (Sanssouci)
May 15th–Oct. 15th Tues.–Sun.
10–12.30 and 13–17, Tel: 96 94 224
Babelsberg Palace (Park Babels-
berg), April–Oct. Tues. – Sun.
10–17, Tel: 96 94 250
Caputh Palace
14548 Caputh, May 15th–Oct. 15th
Tues.–Sun. 10–17, Oct. 16th– May
14th Sat./Sun. 10–16
Tel: 033209-70 345
Cecilienhof Palace (New Garden)
April–Oct. Tues.–Sun. 9–17
Nov.–March Tues.–Sun. 10–16
Tel: 96 24 244
Charlottenhof Palace (Sanssouci)
May 15th–Oct. 15th Tues.–Thurs.
10–12.30 and 13–17, Tel: 96 94 228
Sanssouci Palace
April–Oct. Tues.–Sun. 9–17
Nov. –March Tues.–Sun. 9–12.30
Tel: 96 94 190
Town painting collection
Benkertstrasse 3, Sat.–Thurs. 10–18,
Tel: 281 47 90

Foundation for Prussian Palaces and
Gardens Berlin-Brandenburg
Visitor centre, Postfach 601462,
14414 Potsdam, Tel: 96 94 202,
www.spsg.de
On the history of Glienicker Bridge
Berliner Strasse 98-101,
Mon.–Thurs. 9–16, Fr. 9–13
Leisure
Babelsberger Film Studios
August-Bebel-Strasse 26-53,
entrance Grossbeerenstrasse, March
17th–June 30th 10–18, July 1st–
August 30th 10–20, Sept. 1st–Nov.
4th 10–18, Tel: 721 27 55, 01805-
346666 www.filmpark.de
Film Museum
Marstall/Schlossstrasse 1, daily
10–18, various exhibitions,
Tel: 272 81 18/28
Hans Otto Theater
Am alten Markt, Tel: 98 11 8,
E-mail:ticket-service@hot.potsdam.de,
Internet: www.hot.potsdam.de
Potsdam White Fleet
Lange Brücke, Tel: 275 92 10
Kino Melodie (cinema)
Friedrich-Ebert-Strasse 12,
Tel: 620 06 99
Cinema in Film Museum
Tel: 27 18 10
www.filmmuseum-potsdam.de
Kabarett Obelisk (cabaret)
Charlotten Strasse 31, Tel: 29 10 69
After 8
ArtSpeicher, live music
Zeppelinstrasse 136, Tel: 98 15 0
B-West, station pub
Zeppelinstrasse 146 (in Charlotten-
hof station)
Gutenberg 100, music pub
Gutenbergstrasse 100/102
Internet:www.artspeicher.de
concert box office,
Tel: 96 94 250, 96 94 0
Lindenpark (live music)
Stahnsdorfer Strasse 76-78
Tel: 747 97 0
Liquor Store, Bar
Friedrich-Ebert-Strasse 30
Nikolaisaal
Wilhelm-Staab-Strasse 10/11
Tel: 28 8888 28, Fax: 28 888 22
Waschhaus (music, theatre, film,
exhibitions)
Schiffbauergasse 1, Tel: 271 56 0,
Fax: 280 48 36
E-mail: mail@waschhaus.de
Internet: www.waschhaus.de

Index